T0120626

Recounting God's Faithfulness

PHIL *and* JOYCE
RENICKS

WESTBOW
PRESS®
A DIVISION OF THOMAS NELSON
& ZONDERVAN

Copyright © 2022 Phil and Joyce Renicks.

All rights reserved. No part of this book may be used or reproduced by any means,
graphic, electronic, or mechanical, including photocopying, recording, taping or by
any information storage retrieval system without the written permission of the author
except in the case of brief quotations embodied in critical articles and reviews.

This book is a work of non-fiction. Unless otherwise noted, the author and the publisher
make no explicit guarantees as to the accuracy of the information contained in this book and
in some cases, names of people and places have been altered to protect their privacy.

WestBow Press books may be ordered through booksellers or by contacting:

WestBow Press
A Division of Thomas Nelson & Zondervan
1663 Liberty Drive
Bloomington, IN 47403
www.westbowpress.com
844-714-3454

Because of the dynamic nature of the Internet, any web addresses or links contained
in this book may have changed since publication and may no longer be valid. The views
expressed in this work are solely those of the author and do not necessarily reflect the views
of the publisher, and the publisher hereby disclaims any responsibility for them.

Any people depicted in stock imagery provided by Getty Images are models,
and such images are being used for illustrative purposes only.
Certain stock imagery © Getty Images.

Scripture quotations marked (RSV) are from Revised Standard Version of the Bible,
copyright © 1946, 1952, and 1971 National Council of the Churches of Christ in the
United States of America. Used by permission. All rights reserved worldwide.

Scripture quotations marked (NIV) are taken from the Holy Bible, New International Version®,
NIV®. Copyright © 1973, 1978, 1984, 2011 by Biblica, Inc.® Used by permission of Zondervan.
All rights reserved worldwide. www.zondervan.com The "NIV" and "New International Version"
are trademarks registered in the United States Patent and Trademark Office by Biblica, Inc.®

Scripture quotations marked (NLT) are taken from the Holy Bible, New Living Translation,
copyright ©1996, 2004, 2015 by Tyndale House Foundation. Used by permission of
Tyndale House Publishers, Carol Stream, Illinois 60188. All rights reserved.

ISBN: 978-1-6642-5231-8 (sc)
ISBN: 978-1-6642-5230-1 (e)

Print information available on the last page.

WestBow Press rev. date: 12/16/2021

DEDICATION

To our four amazing children, Marshall, Melissa, Michaela and Matthew and their spouses, our grandchildren and all great grandchildren and future offspring that will come from our loving relationship that began on August 24, 1963.

"A people who have not pride to record their history will not long have the virtues to make history worth recording and no people who are indifferent to their past need hope to make their future great." Virgil A. Lewis

GENERATIONS

My people (children), hear my teaching; listen to the words of my mouth. ² I will open my mouth with a parable; I will utter hidden things, things from of old—³ things we have heard and known, things our ancestors have told us. ⁴ We will not hide them from their descendants; we will tell the next generation the praiseworthy deeds of the LORD, his power, and the wonders he has done. ⁵ He decreed statutes for Jacob and established the law in Israel, which he commanded our ancestors to teach their children, ⁶ so the next generation would know them, even the children yet to be born, and they in turn would tell their children. ⁷ Then they would put their trust in God and would not forget his deeds but would keep his commands.

Psalm 78:1-7 NIV

INTRODUCTION

A Trilogy

ONE OF THE realities that all newlyweds face is the fact that you aren't just marrying each other but you also marry each other's family. Joyce and I both feel blessed, much loved and strongly supported by the families that we married into. Our wedding photo above was taken on August 24, 1963, at the Community Alliance Church on Main Street in Butler, PA. The photo not only symbolizes our marriage to each other, but our love for our ancestral families, the Armitages and the Renicks.

Our wedding photo also symbolizes the format for telling of our life story. The dictionary defines the word 'trilogy' as, "three dramas that are closely related and develop into one theme" and believe me there has been plenty enough drama to go around. *Our Family Story* is the story of three families: The Cassius Armitage Family, the Samuel Renicks Family and of course the Phil and Joyce Renicks family. The central theme of all three families was and is LOVE—Love for Christ, Love for others and Love for each other. And over the love we have for each other is God's overarching FAITHFULNESS

Joyce and I hope and pray that those of our present generation and all future generations to come will not only be inspired by *Our Family Story* but will write the story of your own family. Philip Renicks, 21 September 2015

I

Joyce's Family Story

The Armitage Family

EARLY YEARS OF the Armitage Family

Nestled in the beautiful green rolling hills of Western Pennsylvania is the small town of Corry. This is the town where my story begins. Family legend agrees that William Armitage held the title of High Sheriff of York, England, and along with his two brothers oversaw the bodyguards of King George III (1738-1820). Due to finding themselves out of favor with the king, the three brothers had to flee for their lives and made passage to New York where William married Sylvia Thurston. He was the father of Isaac Armitage, born 1803; Isaac was the father of John, born 1824; John was the father of George Wilber, born 1861; and George Wilber was the father of Owen Burnell Armitage, (OB) born 1894. He was my grandfather.

My grandfather was one of five boys; William, Victor, Lawrence and Harold were his brothers and two sisters, Gladys and Ava. They all lived in the countryside surrounding the small town of Corry. The two sisters and one brother lived in Corry while three of the brothers bought large farms in the outlying areas. Their farms were located on Oil Creek Road, which was the road from Spring Creek to Titusville. Their farms stretched for about eight miles consecutively to Cobbs Corners, which was a four corners road with a small white church on one side and a two-story house behind it. During my father's growing up years, this church was closed. When my father and his brother, Wilson, became of age, they bought farms on the opposite side of the road close to my grandparents. Beyond the church on the same road there were three more farms that belonged to the Cobb brothers, one of which was my grandmother's father. There were lots of fun-filled family gatherings on these farms. My grandfather graduated from high school, which in his day was unheard of for farm boys.

Joyce's Paternal Grandparents
Owen Burnell and Nina Cobb Armitage

My grandmother, Nina Cobb Armitage had one sister, Sarah and one brother, Rowland. Grandma and her sister Sarah married brothers, Owen and Lawrence Armitage. Grandma's brother owned the family farm, a large dairy farm on the same road. I remember visiting the farm and playing in the large front yard. My grandfather was a gentle soft-spoken man who was kind and well liked in the community. My grandmother was a short little woman who was very feisty and not afraid of anyone or anything. They had six children: Wilson, Rolland (Cassius), Elizabeth, Harland, Wilma and Alice. Wilma and Alice were quite a few years younger than the other four. In fact, they were only seven and eight years older than me, so it was like we grew up together. They were so special to me. My father was very sickly as a baby and even though my grandmother never went to church, she prayed to God and promised that if dad lived, she would give him to God to be a preacher.

The McCray Family

Joyce's Maternal Grandparents
Paul and Nellie Jerome McCray

My mother's parents were Paul Burt McCray and Nellie Elva Jerome McCray. My grandfather was born in Spartansburg, Pennsylvania on February 21, 1895. My grandmother was born in Ainsworth, Nebraska on Nov. 10, 1899. Her family was part of a group of settlers on the plains known as 'sodbusters.', the first settlers to arrive on the plains who began to break up the thick prairie sod. They cut thick blocks of sod to build their homes, so she grew up living in a sod house. My grandmother always claimed that Jenny Jerome (Winston Churchill's mother) was a distant relative. Because I was always getting in trouble at school for talking so much, she used to tease me about being like him.

In 1913 her family moved to Spartansburg, where she met my grandfather. They were married on Feb. 20, 1918. They settled on a small farm on the outskirts of Spartansburg, which is about 25 miles from Spring Creek. My grandfather had a sugar bush (a grove of sugar maple trees) on this farm where he made pure maple syrup. I loved to go out to the sugar bush with him. It was fascinating to watch him collect the buckets that held the sap from the trees. He would pour it into a large cooking pot that hung above a wood fire in a small shack where he cooked and stirred the sap. It took several hours, and he would have to keep going out to stir it and check it to see when it had cooked down to the right consistency. Once it was cooked, he poured it into metal tins. We had pure maple syrup for our pancakes all my growing up years.

My grandparents had three children, Grace, Margaret Ellen and Walter. They later sold that farm and my grandfather bought a service station and garage in Spartansburg. The garage had two apartments over the top of it and that is where my grandparents lived in one and Uncle Walter and his family lived in the other until they had four children and then it was too small. My grandfather McCray was fun-loving and at holidays he would make a big sawdust pile and bury lots of pennies in it. When he would say "Go," all the grandchildren would try to find as many pennies as we could. I still have fond memories of that.

He had been a square dance caller and would often do that for us grandchildren. My grandmother was very fussy about her house and we were never allowed to sit on her living room furniture. Most of the time when we would go for a visit, we would play downstairs in grandpa's garage. It was an exceptionally large garage where he would work on cars. There was a pit to drive cars over with lots of cars sitting around that he was working on. We had lots of fun playing hide and seek.

My grandfather McCray also owned several school busses that bused the kids to school in Spartansburg and Corry. He also was an inventor of sorts. I am sure that some of the things he invented could have been sold if he had gotten a patent for them. One concoction I distinctly remember was a thick black medicine that if put on sores, burns, wounds, etc., it would pull the poison out. Since it didn't have a name, we always called it "sticky medicine." Mom always had a large bottle of it on hand when we were growing up.

Love – Marriage – Baby Carriage

My parents met at an April Fools party given by mutual friends where my dad proceeded to lean against a sewing machine that had a pin cushion on top of it and he had many pins and needles sticking in his backside. He took a lot of good-natured teasing due to that. Since my parents didn't have a

Joyce's Dad, Rolland
Cassius Armitage

church, they eloped and went to Burlington, Kentucky where they were married. My grandfather begged them not to get married on a Friday as he believed anything that happened on Friday never lasted, but they didn't have enough money to stay in two hotel rooms that night so they found a justice of the peace who married them on Friday March 22, 1941.

They began their married life as farmers. Dad was exempt from the service during World War II (1941-45) as the country needed farmers to grow crops for food. I was born June 18, 1942, in Corry Hospital. I was my grandma Armitage's first grandchild and was always accused of being her favorite.

In 1946 Bill and Mae Conley moved to Spartansburg to start a Christian and Missionary Alliance church. My grandmother McCray felt sorry for them because the church was small, so she started attending. She decided to take me to Sunday school. My parents had to bring me from the farm to her house. After a short while

Joyce's Mom, Margaret
Ellen McCray Armitage

they decided to attend the church as well. This church is where they met the Lord as their Savior. My parents and the Conley's became particularly good friends and remained close even though the Conley's left Spartansburg shortly after that to become C&MA missionaries to Indonesia. They kept in contact by letters and visits when the Conley's were home on furlough.

My sister Carol Jean was born on March 31, 1945. I don't have a lot of memories of these years except Carol and I had the measles at the same time and had to stay in a darkened room for a few days. One day she was playing with a sharp knife and I tried to take it away from her and sliced my middle finger wide open. There was blood everywhere in the kitchen. I remember

Joyce's Dad with Joyce and Carol at the Park

Carol 2 Joyce 4

that my mom fainted at the doctor's office while he was stitching up my finger. My sister Carol died when she was almost two with pneumonia on Jan. 17, 1947. I remember clearly when my parents told me. I was sitting at the dining room table at my grandmother's house coloring with my Aunt Alice and Aunt Wilma when my parents walked in the room. The original plan had been that they would stay at the hospital all night and I was going to stay at Grandma's. When they walked in the door my grandmother said, "Oh no" and she started to cry. Then my parents told me that she had died. I am not sure how much I really comprehended at that point, but I was disappointed that I couldn't stay all night with Grandma.

I don't remember much about the funeral although my mother told me that when I saw Carol for the first time in the casket, I thought she was sleeping and told the funeral director that she needed her doll. He told me to bring it and they put it in the casket with her. I vividly remember the burial at the cemetery looking down at the closed casket. It was such a cold day and I remember thinking that she was going to be very cold in the ground. I always said that when I had a daughter, I was going to name her after Carol. I didn't get to name a daughter Carol, but Michaela has her middle name Jean.

Dad's Call to Ministry

My sister Beverly Ann was born on June 1, 1947, six months after Carol died. During the next year, my dad felt the call of God on his life to go into full time ministry as a preacher, (remember my grandmother's promise to God 25 years earlier). My brother Ronald Cassius (Ron) was born 13 months after Bev on July 11, 1948. That fall we moved to Toccoa Falls, Georgia for Dad to attend Toccoa Falls Bible College. It was my first year of school. I went to school in a small red brick schoolhouse on the edge of campus. I do not have fond memories of that school as we had to eat the lunch the school provided, which was black-eyed peas and cornbread every day. Since I grew up in the north and had never eaten either one before I didn't like them. We couldn't go outside to play until we had cleaned our plate, so I rarely got to go out to play except on the day that we had pork-n-beans and white bread, which was once a month.

It was a hard year for our family, having been used to living in a large farmhouse. The first semester we lived in a small trailer and second semester we lived in married couples housing, which consisted of a combination small kitchen and living room and one bedroom. Mom and Dad slept in a double bed in the corner, Bev and I slept in bunk beds and Ron slept in a crib. My parents made many wonderful life-long friends with the families that lived in the same housing.

After that year we moved back to the farm as Dad had run out of money and needed to save for the rest of his schooling. Looking back it seems ironic that my grandpa Armitage didn't loan dad the money to finish. I suspect it was because he was so angry that my dad would leave farming to go into the ministry.

I went to West Spring Creek School for second grade. This was also the year that I accepted Christ as my Savior at home with mom and dad.

My brother Dale Allen was born on August 19, 1950, just before my dad was to go to Nyack Missionary College, in New York (a lot closer to home} to finish up his schooling.

Dale was a sickly baby and almost died while still in the hospital so it was decided that Dad would go to Nyack by himself for the first semester and then we would all join him in January. He was so homesick for his family that he came back after a month and said he had found a house to rent for all of us, so we packed up and moved to West Nyack. My dad then sold the farm to Aunt Elizabeth and Uncle Ronald. I went to school in Nanuet for third grade. My memories are of having to rock Dale a lot so Mom could do some of her work.

Dad was gone to classes during the day as he was trying to do two years in one as this was a three-year degree. We lived close to New York City and the threat of a nuclear attack from the Russians seemed imminent. This was during the Cold War, a time of great tension between the United States and Russia who were on the brink of nuclear war. We had to take canned goods to school. They were stored in an underground space where there was enough food stored to feed all the students for several days. The school would have air raid drills so we would know exactly how to evacuate to that space.

Dad was able to finish his degree in that year and he felt the Lord calling him back to Spring Creek to open the small church at Cobbs Corners that had been closed for many years. To make ends meet Dad bought a 100-acre farm about a mile down the road from the original farm he owned. We had dairy cows, pigs, chickens and of course a collie dog for a pet. He opened the church and started preaching while tending the farm. Dad was a hard worker. My sister, Deborah Lee, was born that year on November 4, 1951.

There was no one who could play the piano for the church services so Dad had me take piano lessons and he asked the teacher to teach me how to play hymns as soon as possible; therefore, I still play the piano but mostly hymns. So, I became the piano player. Very few people came at first, but dad's family came to support him and they soon all came to faith in Christ. During the next seven years, dad continued to pastor the church and saw it grow. It now had a Sunday School, youth group, Sunday morning and evening services and Wednesday night prayer meeting. The church was accepted into the Christian and Missionary Alliance and my dad received his ordination in 1955.

While living on the farm my dad had led an older man named Eddie Johnson to the Lord. Eddie was well known in the community as a hard worker who hired himself out to various farmers. Dad needed a full time hired hand to help with the farm chores since dad was also preaching, and he hired Eddie. We soon discovered that Eddie couldn't read or write. My mom taught him to write his name. He loved the Lord so much that God answered his prayer to be able to read the Bible. He couldn't read anything else. What a miracle for me to witness this as a young child. He lived with us for several years.

In 1957 my parents sold the farm to my Aunt Grace and Uncle Dick and bought a house right next to the church. Because Dad lived on a free will offering, he took a job as a school bus driver to supplement his income. My Dad was a fun-loving person who loved to laugh so he was well liked and respected by people of all ages. My closest friends were in the youth group. I keep in contact with Janet Burleigh (Moravek) and Jack Moravek. We played a lot of games when we got together and playing baseball was a favorite. I was an incredibly good baseball player.

In the winter we had snow! Lots of snow! We spent countless hours together sled riding, having snowball fights and bobsled riding (our favorite). Because we lived near Lake Erie, we had winter with snow from October through April. We all went to school and rode the same bus together as well. At the end of the school year, Dad would take all the kids from his school

Joyce and her mom on top of a snowbank in front of their house

bus route to an amusement park for a day to Conneaut Lake Park. We had so much fun riding the rides; the roller coaster was my favorite ride which I would ride several times.

In 1956 dad was approached by a group of people who attended a small struggling church called Excelsior, about 20 miles down the road closer to Titusville. The church was without a pastor so he started preaching there as well. The churches would stagger Sunday school and church on Sunday morning and take turns on Sunday night. So now he had two prayer meetings during the week and later he had two youth groups. We went to a lot of church activities. Besides taking care of us, my mom was a faithful worker and helpmeet to my dad. She also was a lot of fun and loved by all.

Joyce's Growing Up Years

My growing up years were carefree and happy. Because my parents were young and so much fun, all my friends wanted to come to my house. I finished my grade school years at West Spring Creek, and I started going to Corry High School when I was in seventh grade. We entered it as the first class in a new school. I rode the bus to school. I loved school and had a lot of friends.

I also loved living on the farm and in the country. One of my favorite times of the year was when we would cut the hay, bail it in rectangular bales and take it to the barn to store for the cows. I would drive the tractor while the men loaded the bales of hay on the wagon or I would ride on the bailer and watch the twine as it came out and wound around the bales to be sure it was good and tight. To this day, when I smell hay cut in the fields it brings back so many happy memories.

We had dairy cows that would be lined up in the stanchions in the barn where they were milked, and they stayed in at night or in really bad weather. Whenever I had to give a speech or talk at school, I would go out to the barn and stand in front of the line of cows and practice it. They were good listeners and they would moo to tell me it was well done. All my family would make fun of me. I also liked to bring the cows in from the field in the late afternoon to be milked. I never milked the cows, but I sometimes watched my dad.

A group of C&MA pastors in our area started a family camp in Edinboro, Pennsylvania. Pastors in that area and their families did all the work of running the weeklong camp. We worked hard, but we also had a lot of fun. Our family always stayed in a large room upstairs in the farmhouse. Our whole family slept in one room over the kitchen. One time, my sister Beve opened one of the dresser drawers to find that a mouse had made a nest and had babies in her underwear. The downstairs contained the kitchen and dining room. There was always a big group of young people from the Erie C&MA Tabernacle and I made a lot of great friends: Larry and Nada Loomis, Joan Vargo, Donnie Huntingdon and Dave Bloom.

Bill Nickolas was our youth leader. He and his wife later went overseas as Alliance missionaries to Indonesia and then worked at the C&MA

headquarters in Colorado. The afternoons were free, so we would go swimming and canoeing on Edinboro Lake, play ping pong and play all kinds of pranks on some of the pastors. A youth camp sprung up at the same site, which is where I met Woody Stemple, Larry Kaiser and Mae and Dolly Wolfe. It was amazing how many of us ended up going to Nyack together. These camps were held in August. Edinboro Camp will always hold a special place in my heart.

My grandparents (Armitage) were the first people in our family to get a television so every Friday night we went to their house to watch "Life of Riley," a comedy show that aired on NBC. Grandma would always serve Neapolitan ice cream that she would slice. She never served anything different. How we loved it.

I don't remember much about my dad's brother Harland who joined the Air Force as soon as he graduated from high school. He never came back home to live. He usually came to visit once a year. He was stationed in the South, where he met my Aunt Katherline who was from Montgomery, Alabama, so they settled in the South. My Uncle fought in World War II as a pilot and made a career in the Air Force. Interestingly, he went on to graduate from Auburn University. He and Aunt Katherine had three girls: Kaye, Sherri and Lisa. When he retired from the Air Force, he went to work for Lockheed Martin.

Uncle Wilson married Frances and they had five children: Sharon, Milton, Kathy, Barbara and Roger. They lived on a farm next to my grandparents when we were all quite young. My uncle became a Baptist preacher and they moved away when we were in middle school.

My Aunt Elizabeth was married to Walter Damon and they had a daughter, Nadine. He also served in World War II as a pilot and was killed on his last flight before coming home. His plane went down over England on a flight back from Germany, but his crew bailed out and survived. A few years later, she married Ronald Messenger and they bought a farm up the hill from my grandparents (it was the first farm that my parents had owned). They had a son, Paul. Uncle Ronald was a farmer and a very mean, abusive man, while also being very lazy. My aunt had to work awfully hard on the farm. He tried to talk like he was the best Christian there ever was. I did not like him and really was afraid of him. Years later, I found out that he had physically and sexually abused my cousin Nadine. She ran away from home with a neighbor boy who she married when they graduated high school and never came back.

My two youngest aunts both married the same year. Aunt Wilma married Frank Ross (he had served in the Navy) and they left to go to Nyack Missionary College. They later went to Irian Jaya as missionaries with the C&MA in 1960. They had three children; Ramon, Donna and Joleen. They served in Pyramid and Sentani, Irian Jaya. My aunt had real blond hair and they thought she was a goddess.

Aunt Alice married Dale Jones (who was a Marine) and they lived in Edinboro, Pennsylvania where Uncle Dale taught school and later became an administrator. They had three children: Kerry, Marlene and Diane. I was 16 when Kerry was born. They later moved to the Philadelphia area, where the kids all settled.

Mom's older sister, Grace, married Dick Lincoln and they had five children: Larry, Sharon, Duane, Evelyn and Grace. Uncle Dick was a very mean man and beat the kids unmercifully when he was angry. Sharon was six months older than me, so we were quite close all through my growing up years. She went to Toccoa Falls Bible College and met her husband there. They settled in the Orlando area, so I didn't see her much after that.

Mom's brother Walter served in the Navy as a cook on a ship. He married Dottie and they had four children: Michael, Michelle, Kevin and Kim. I never knew these cousins as they were so much younger than me. Walter and Grandpa McCray ran the Mobil service station and garage in Spartansburg for several years, then he and his family moved to Corry, where he was a mechanic. Uncle Walter was a fun person, but never went to church or professed the Lord as his Savior.

Sometime in the 1960s, my Grandpa McCray sold the garage and bought a piece of land between Spartansburg and Corry. They had an artisan well that was capped to make a fountain that sprayed high into the air. The water flowed into a pond that grandpa stocked with fish. They put a mobile home on the property and moved there. Grandpa died of a heart attack in 1965 while he was deer hunting on the property. Grandma later married Leon McCray, who was grandpa's cousin. He was a gentle kind man.

Move to Oil City, Pennsylvania

In 1958, Dad felt the call of God to leave Cobbs Corners and move to Oil City, Pennsylvania to preach in the C&MA church. He sold our house to the church for a parsonage and we moved the day before school started. It was my junior year. I did not want to move and leave all my friends. The next two years were the worst years of my life. Oil City is an old, dirty oil town that had five oil refineries close by so there was a sulfur smell that hung over the city; in the summer, the smell was so thick you could taste it. The school was an old school on three levels, and you could enter each level from the ground as it was built on a steep hill. I had to walk almost two miles to school by myself at first. How I hated that. I did make one girlfriend that walked to school with me. I took the secretarial and business course. I also took two years of Spanish Both of which would come in handy later in life. I enjoyed my classes, but that was all that I liked. I didn't make many friends and the young people in the church were either older or younger. Since my next sibling, Beve, was five years younger we weren't close either. I wrote lots of letters to my friends in Corry and went back every chance I could. I was lonely.

I met Joanne Whitling at the church in Oil City, and she would later become my roommate at Nyack. She was five years older than me, so was not a part of the youth group. She had a good job as a secretary and had a car so occasionally we would do something together. She was a lot of fun.

Now that we were in a different area, we didn't go to Edinboro Camp. We went to Mahaffey Camp near Punxsutawney, Pennsylvania. Mahaffey was quite different, but I have some great memories of fun times there. The main difference was that there were no flushing toilets in the whole place, so we had to use outdoor toilets that were located at different areas in the park. Mom and Dad bought a small cottage close to the main tabernacle with a porch with swings. We could sit on the swings and hear the service in the tabernacle. I worked in the kitchen and although we worked a lot, we made it fun and I got to know a lot of the pastors in that area.

All the youth groups from the area C&MA churches would gather once a month on a Saturday night for a youth rally with a social time. That was where I met' Don Reitz from Franklin, Pennsylvania. We dated a few times, but he was a little too arrogant to suit me. I graduated from Oil City High School on June 6, 1960. Oh, Happy Day!

My father received a free will offering from the people of the church so my parents never knew from week to week how much money they would get to live on. I have heard my parents tell a lot of stories of how God was faithful and met all their needs. If we were poor, we kids were never aware of it. My folks never gave the impression that we didn't have the money to do things because Dad was a preacher. They never bought anything on credit. They even paid cash for the car when they bought a new one. My parents lived by faith and we kids saw a lot of answered prayers during our growing up years. My parents also lived what my dad preached, so I saw demonstrated the way a Christian should walk and talk.

We didn't have a TV until my first year of college, so our family played lots of board games. Our favorite was Monopoly and we would play for hours. My brother Dale would hide most of his money up his pant legs and we would feel sorry for him since he didn't have much money. We would not always charge him rent on properties we owned, then he would win. We would fall for it every time.

College Years

After graduating high school, I was accepted at Nyack Missionary College and Toccoa Falls Bible College, but I chose to go to Nyack because it was closer to home and I felt that was where God wanted me to go. I left for Nyack Missionary College, Nyack, New York in September 1960. Nyack is a school of the Christian and Missionary Alliance located on a beautiful hillside overlooking the Hudson River and the Tappan Zee Bridge. There were approximately 500 students. I am sure my parents didn't have the money for me to go, but they didn't stop me, and they were able to make all the payments. Joanne Whitling decided to go at the last minute. We became roommates and June McHenry from Aliquippa was the third roommate. Joanne was a fun roommate and June was quiet. We got along well considering that there were three girls in a room designed for two.

The girl's dorm was called Christie Hall. Our room consisted of bunk beds and a single bed with two small dressers and 2 small desks. We also had two small closets so to say we were crowded was an understatement.

None of us had a lot of clothes so we managed. We shared a bathroom with 15 girls. It had three toilet stalls, a tub and a separate shower. What fun especially on date nights of big events. We had a weeknight curfew of 9 o'clock and 11 o'clock on weekends. We had to sign out, putting what time we left and where we were going if we went off campus. We then would have to sign in when we returned. We were required to go to chapel every day  and we had assigned seats alphabetically. I always sat beside Phil's roommate Sid Ballou, so we got to be good friends.

We were also required to go to Friday night missionary meeting – this was the big date night of the week. Everyone was always checking to see who had a date and with whom. We had to sign an attendance slip every week on Monday as to the days we attended chapel and missionary meeting. We also were required to go to church every Sunday on campus. We had an assigned table to sit at every evening meal, which was served family style. There were no choices for food – you either ate what they had or didn't eat. Breakfast and lunch were served cafeteria style and again we had no choices. We wore dresses to everything and hats on Sunday mornings. I guess that is where I developed my love for hats. Even though we had all these rules, we had a lot of fun and I loved being at Nyack.

My Dad's advice to me when I left for Nyack was to study hard my first two years and then the last two have more of a social life. Nyack was often called "Simpson's matchbox" as many people met their spouse there. A. B. Simpson was the founder. I had gone to Nyack thinking that I wouldn't know anybody and was surprised at how many of my friends from Edinboro were there. It was great to be with them.

I had to study hard as I had taken the secretarial/business course in high school so was not prepared for the more academic challenges of writing papers. I didn't do well at writing papers, but I did well on tests and the rest of the work, so my grades were above average. The girls that I hung out with and who became my closest friends were Pam Hoover Heim, Diane Schroder Zimmerman, Pris Retallack Wilson, Dale Womack Stump, Joanne Whitling and Judy Simmons Fields. Since there were only about 90 in our class and 500 in the whole school, I got to know most of the students there and was friends with most of them. I knew Phil from being in class with him, but never did much with him as he had a girlfriend back home.

The very first date that I had was arranged by my friend Woody Stemple. We went into New York City to hear Dr. Billy Graham speak at a large crusade in Madison Square Garden. I was so excited to be able to hear him in such a large place and to see him in person, as he looked much like my dad. It was like seeing dad up there on the stage. I didn't date much that year as I was too busy studying and doing things with my girlfriends. Nobody in our class had cars so most of our social activities were done in groups of friends.

While I was at home during Easter vacation that year, my Grandpa Armitage died on Easter Day, 1961. It was very sudden as he had a heart attack in bed and died before anyone could get there to help him. This was an incredibly sad time and I stayed home an extra week so I could go to the funeral. My grandma sold the farm shortly after that and went to live with Aunt Alice and her family. Grandma would stay with each one of her kids for a month or more each year, so she wasn't a burden to Aunt Alice. She gave her TV to my parents so that was the first TV we had.

I was a counselor at Edinboro Camp for several weeks that summer of 1961 which was quite different from being a participant and worker. Little did I know that would be the last time that I would go to Edinboro Camp. One evening when we were having a picnic supper for the participants, the counselors were serving the food (grilled hot dogs, chips, etc.) We would fix the plate, give it to the person and they would put what condiments they wanted on it. When all the kids were served, the counselors got their food and when I opened my bun to put the ketchup on my hotdog, it was a whole dead fish with its eye looking right at me. Of course, I screamed and threw the sandwich, which everyone thought was so funny. For once, the prank was on me.

At the end of that summer (1961) my family moved to Butler, Pennsylvania, where Dad was to be the pastor at the C&MA church. We moved just before I went back to Nyack for my second year. Dad pastored the Butler Alliance Church for 18 years and moved the church twice and built the new campus on Mercer Road.

That year I started working at the school library part time. I really liked the job, even though my boss, Miss Speidel, was a typical librarian (always admonishing the students to be quiet). I didn't mind working for her and I loved Bea Turner and Lois Long who worked with me. The library was in Shuman Hall and occasionally, I would work at the front desk where students checked their books in and out. I got to know a lot of students that way. Sometimes I had to close the library at night and walk back to the dorm in the dark. That was a bit scary. I dated a little bit more that semester, but still had too much fun with friends to get serious.

Shuman Hall Library where Joyce worked

When I came back from Christmas vacation, I found out that Phil had broken up with his girlfriend back home so that meant he was available. He immediately started dating some girls in our class so at that point we were still just friends. It crossed my mind a couple of times that I would like to date him as he was tall and good looking, but back then a girl never asked a boy for a date or even let him know she was interested.

One night we had a concert at the school where Bev Shea (famous soloist for Billy Graham) was the soloist. Our school had invited The King's College, another Christian college in the area to come so we knew it was going to be crowded. To get good seats, we seven girls skipped supper and went into the auditorium to claim our seats. When we got to the row we wanted, there were books in several seats on one end. It left one seat short for us so one of my girlfriends moved the books from one seat to across the aisle. We sat down and I was the one who was sitting by the empty seat with books. When the owners of the books came to claim their seats, they were not happy about what we had done, but I wasn't about to move as I had sat there all through the supper hour. As it turned out, Phil sat beside me and after he got over being upset with us, he started talking to me. It was a moving concert and I enjoyed sitting by him very much.

Our Dating Relationship

On Feb. 24, 1962, Phil asked me out for our first date and the rest is history. We went to the Nyack basketball game, then walked down the hill to the Hilltop Bar and Restaurant, to get pizza which was strictly off limits to Nyack students. They had live music and he requested my favorite song, "Five Foot Two Eyes of Blue." As we walked, I held Phil up as it was a snowy icy night and he was wearing leather soled shoes. We pretty much dated exclusively after that. Now that we were a couple, we did a lot of things with other couples. Our best friends were Chip and Muriel, Sid and Dixie, Pam and Lowell, Paul and Dale and Bob and Sharon. Our first kiss was in April and when he went to kiss me just before we went into the dorm his coat collar got between our lips and we hardly kissed. That was good for a laugh.

His parents came to pick him up at the end of the school year, so that was when I met them. At first, I thought his dad must be his grandfather! They gave me a ride to Butler where Phil and they met my parents and siblings. Phil drove over a few times during the summer and I went to visit him and meet his Aunt Mary and Uncle Ed, Faye, Rue and Vicki Wittlinger. Before I left, I prayed and asked the Lord that he would show me during this time if Phil was the one for me. I remembered back to Mahaffy Camp just a few weeks before where I dedicated myself to missionary service. I was willing to break-up with Phil if that was what God wanted. If Phil was to be the one, he would need to say something about wanting to serve God overseas. I had never told him that was what I wanted to do. One evening he proceeded to tell me that he felt the call of God to be a missionary. It was then and there I knew that it was what the Lord wanted for both of us.

He showed me all around Zanesville and I had my first visit to Tom's Ice Cream Bowl. Our junior year we studied hard and did a lot of fun things with our friends. He gave me my diamond on Dec. 12, 1962, on top of the mountain overlooking the Tappan Zee Bridge on the Hudson River. It was a beautiful night. By the time he gave it to me, it was time for my curfew. I didn't know that he had asked for special permission for me to stay out late. I was so excited and couldn't wait to go home to show my parents. Early spring, at a little Italian pizza joint in Congers, NY we decided that we wanted to get married that summer. We began making plans and looking for an apartment. We found a second floor one-bedroom apartment on South Highland Ave. We didn't want to live in the married couples' apartments if we could find something else. The rest of the year went fast, and we went home to get jobs and make some money. We had set the date for our wedding to be August 24th.

II

Phil's Family Story

The Renicks Family

MY FATHER, SAMUEL George Renicks, was born in Ambridge, Pennsylvania, April 29, 1911. My mother Martha Virginia (Brock) Renicks was born in Zanesville, Ohio, July 28, 1917.

I, Philip Marshall Renicks, was born at Bethesda Hospital in Zanesville on July 8, 1942. I have one sibling, Stephen Alan Renicks, born October 16, 1948 in Zanesville, Ohio.

My grandparents William and Elizabeth Renicks were both living when I was born. I'm pictured here with my grandmother Renicks when I was just a year old. She was

a godly woman. I really never knew her because she passed away on August 4, 1944, less than a month after my 2nd birthday. She was born on August 22, 1875 in Uphall, West Lothian, Scotland. She was the daughter of John Marshall and Jane Thornton Marshall, both born in Scotland in 1851. My great grandfather was born in Uphall and my great grandmother was born in Airth Stirlingshire, where they were married on December 5, 1873. My grandfather Renicks, William, was born on July 1, 1874. He and my grandmother married in Broxburn, Scotland in June 1903. My aunt Jean Thornton Renicks was born in Broxburn April 19, 1904.

My grandparents immigrated from Scotland to the United States in 1905. My grandfather William was the first to arrive from Scotland to New

Phil's Paternal Grandparents
William and Elizabeth

York at Ellis Island on the ship Caledonia. He left my grandmother and my Aunt Jean behind in Scotland until he could earn enough money to bring them to America. According to the ships manifest of 'Alien Passengers for U.S. Immigration at the Port of Arrival' my grandfather had embarked from Glasgow, on July 15, to arrive in New York on July 23, 1905. He was listed as being from Broxburn, Scotland where he and my grandmother were living at the time.

The ships manifest listed him as a driver; I'm not sure what that means. He had $50 in his pocket. I know that he worked in the steel mills in Coatbridge at one time before he married my grandmother. William and Eliza (Elizabeth) were married on June 22, 1903, by Alex Middleton, Minister of the Parish of Broxburn where they were attending church.

In 1995 Joyce and I had the privilege to visit Scotland. We traveled with the late David Pollock and his wife Betty Lou, dear friends of ours. We searched out and found the church where my grandparents were married. We stood holding hands in the front of the church where my grandparents would have stood when they pledged themselves to each other. We had the address in Coatbridge where my grandfather was born. He was born at home in a row house. The increible story behind finding the location took us into an adjoining neighborhood because of a wrong turn. Frankly we were lost. A man came out of his house to get into his car. I stopped and asked him for directions to the street and the particular address of my grandfathers home. He said, "Follow me, I'm going that way". When we arrived on the street, he stopped along the curb in front of empty lots. All the houses were gone. He said that the government had torn them down about ten years prior. He asked the surname and when I told him Renicks, he got a surprised look on his face and said, "That was my morther's maiden name". As we talked, we figured out that our grandfathers must have been cousins. What is the likelihood of that happening?

We had an incredible conversation and he suggested that we needed to visit the museum of the Coatbridge Iron Works where my grandfather worked. He said they had preserved an amazing collection of photos and names of the individuals who had worked there. However, time didn't permit. I am still hoping that one day I can return to Scotland.

My grandfather came to the US on the sponsorship of his brother S.A. Renicks, my great uncle Sam. Uncle Sam was a pastor, church planter and established a number of Christian and Missionary Alliance churches in Western Pennsylvania. He held pastorates in Ambridge, New Castle, Corry and Farrell, Pennsylvania. My grandfather came to Ambridge, just outside Pittsburgh and lived with his brother in a section known as Old Economy. He found work at the American Bridge Works. They lived in Old Colony, at 913 Maplewood Ave. Pictured are my dad, Samuel, next to him in back is my Aunt Jean, in front is my uncle Wilfred and on the right is my Aunt Mary.

There were some important milestones along the way in my grandmother's life. I'm not sure when they moved from Ambridge to Zanesville, but I do know that my grandfather made a bad investment and ended up losing most everying they had in savings. It was a difficult time for the family.

My grandmother Renicks, along with a lady by the name of Mother Bowman and ten others, founded the Zanesville, Christian and Missionary Allince Church in 1937. My grandmother Elizabeth became a naturalzed citizen of the United States on June 10, 1938 in Zanesville, at the age of 63. My grandfather was naturalized February 7, 1924 in Ambridge. When they

moved to Zanesville, my dad was 12 years old. They moved to a house on Central Avenue where I can remember several fun times with cousins. Aunt Jean had two girls, Elaine and Evelyn; Uncle Wilfred had two girls Janet and Joy; my dad and mom had two boys; and Aunt Mary and Uncle Ed didn't have children. In many ways they became like a second set of parents for Steve and me.

My parents were blue collar workers in Zanesville, Ohio. My parents had eloped to Wellsburg, West Virginia on

Mom, Martha Virginia
Brock Age 16

November 3, 1933, along with my Uncle Willard (my mom's brother) and his wife Pearl. Uncle Willard drove the getaway car to Wellsburg. I'm sure that my mother knew that her parents would never have approved of her getting married at age 16. She had just finished eighth grade the year before and had dropped out of school to care for her younger sister Myrtle. Dad and mom had decided to live apart but I don't think mom fooled anybody. This separation lasted about a year. Mom went to work to help make ends meet. She worked in a plant owned by the Hoover

Dad at age 22
A Pretty Handsome Dude

Vacuum Cleaner Company that had been turned into a wartime plant where she was responsible to solder fuses for bombs. Because there was the potential for an explosion, she had to put her hands through holes in a very heavy tempered plate glass partition to solder. Mom and Dad were both part of the war effort. The pictures above were taken the year they were married.

If you do the math on my arrival into the world, mom and dad had waited what my mom often described as nine long and painful years to have their first child. My mother had a difficult pregnancy and spent much of the 9 months in bed for fear of losing this baby that they had waited for so long. By the time I was born, my mom and dad were living in a cozy cottage. My grandfather Brock had given my dad a corner of his pasture lot just a few hundred feet down the road from the homestead.

Our house was a three-bedroom home with a kitchen, living room and dining room. We also had indoor plumbing that my grandmother Brock didn't have. When my mom and dad first moved in, they didn't have electricity and used only an oil lamp at night. I keep that oil lamp in my study as a reminder of where I have come from.

Our home was a kit, the prefab Crafton Home from the Sears and Roebuck catalog. The homes ranged in price from $916 to $1,399. I'm quite sure that our home was on the lower end of the scale, but it was still a nice looking home. Sears kit homes were shipped via boxcar and came with a 75-page instruction book. Each kit contained 10,000 - 30,000 pieces and the framing members were all marked to facilitate easy construction.

There are a number of things that I remember about living in that house, although I was only five years old when we moved from there to the farm in Hopewell, ten miles out into the country. There was a lot of yard space to play in, along with a rippling brook in the backyard behind the garage that I loved to explore. We had a big weeping willow tree in the front side yard that provided my mom and dad with a steady supply of willow switches which she thought I needed. I remember one time when my mom emptied the box from the bathroom where my dad kept his used double edged razor blades. She told me she was putting them in the trash barrel in the backyard and I was not to go near them because I would cut myself. Why did she think this was information that I needed? Well, I checked them out and of course I got cut. I remember coming into the house crying and bleeding asking for a bandaid. However, before mom cleaned me up or got me a bandaid I got the willow switch on my bare legs for being disobedient. How cruel is that?

Desperate Times – The War Years

My parents must have wondered what kind of world they had brought me into. It was a desperate time to be born into a world faced with the grim reality of Hitler's German army marching across Europe at will and Japan gobbling up the territory across Asia and the islands of the Pacific. Europe was being ripped apart and by 1942 tens of thousands of American soldiers had joined the Allied troops fighting to stop Hitler's advance across Europe.

The United States had officially entered World War II after the bombing of Pearl Harbor on December 7, 1941. Most of the war effort was concentrated in the Pacific battling the Japanese. In addition, efforts were underway for the United States to join the British forces that were losing badly against Rommel, who was nicknamed the "Desert Fox" in North Africa.

Uncle Ed and the War

Uncle Ed, Edgar Russell McClellan, whom I would become remarkably close to as I got older, officially entered active service in World War II just before I was born. He held the rank of Corporal and was listed as an airplane armorer attached to the 522nd Fighter Squadron SE, 27th Fighter Group. According to his separation record from the US Army, an airplane armorer in the European Theater of Operations performed repair and maintenance on 50-caliber machine guns, bomb racks, bomb release mechanisms, and gun mounts on the P-40, A-36, and the P-47 aircraft. He inspected, disassembled, cleaned, repaired and assembled parts, and loaded bombs on bomb racks of the aircraft prior to a mission.

The following information is a rendering of his military service in North Africa, Sicily, Italy and France as chronicled in a service record book that my Aunt Mary had kept and from his honorable discharge papers from the Army of the United States. The 27th Fighter Group trained in the US, where it was equipped with the A-20 aircraft. Uncle Ed shipped out on December 12, 1942 aboard the James Parker troop ship for a voyage of some 14 days. The ship had been re-outfitted as a troop ship and had space for 2,234 troops. I can't imagine what must have been going through the minds of these men knowing what they were going to face and having 14 days of idle time to think about it.

Uncle Edgar (Ed) McClellan
Corsica Spring 1944

From December 26, 1942, to July 17, 1943, Uncle Ed was stationed in North Africa. In the week before the invasion of Sicily (July 3 – 10, 1943) the 27th attacked Axis supply centers in the south and center of Sicily. Uncle Ed served in Sicily from July 18 to September 12, 1943, before being transferred to Italy, where he remained until July 12, 1944. In August 1943, the group was re-designated as the 27th Fighter-Bomber Group. In September it was used to cover the landings at Salerno (Operation Avalanche), which began on September 9,1943. On September 10, the group was awarded a Distinguished Unit Citation for its part in preventing three German armored divisions from reaching the beachhead.

In May 1944, the group became the 27th Fighter Group. The picture is of Uncle Ed loading belts of ammo on the P-40 Warhawk on Corsica in the spring of 1944. His fighter group moved from Corsica to France where his group supported the Seventh Army invasion of Southern France as it advanced up the Rhone Valley. The group briefly returned to Italy, but early in 1945 it transferred back to France, from which it attacked German communications in northern Italy and supported the Allied invasion of Germany.

During his last tour in Italy, he was injured and was flown to England for medical treatment from March-May 1945 before he was flown back to the US to the Ashburn General Hospital in McKinney, Texas, where he was later discharged on August 16, 1945.

To say the least, I was totally unaware of any of this. I would only learn about it as I got old enough to understand and begin my love of history that would lead me to study and write about World War II and the Yalta Agreement for my senior research paper at Nyack.

Some of the people that Uncle Ed met personally included some of the most prominent figures in American History. : President Franklin D. Roosevelt, General George Patton, General Mark Clark, General Eisenhower and General Montgomery. Other personalities included Pope Pius, and entertainers Ernie Pyle, Bob Hope, Jack Benny and Irving Berlin all who came to cheer the troops.

Brock Family

My mom, Martha Virginia Brock, was born to Charles and Ollie Brock. My grandfather, Charles Edwin Brock was born June 13, 1871 in Chandlersville, Ohio, and my grandmother Ollie Lucas Brock, was born January 29, 1885 in Zanesville, Ohio. They were married on September 25, 1906. Grandpa Brock was 35 and Grandma Brock was 21. The picture to the lower right was their wedding picture. My grandfather Brock died in February of 1942, so I never knew him. He and my grandmother are buried in Greenwood Cemetery, Zanesville, Ohio. When I think about enjoying my grandchildren the way I do, it makes me sad that I never knew my grandfather Brock.

My Grandmother lived just about 1000 feet away on the same dirt road from where my parents had built our little cottage. I got that willow switch more than one time on my bare legs from running off and going to my grandmother's. After all, it was "Grandma's House" and I loved it there. There was

Grandpa and Grandma Brock
Wedding Photo

always so much going on. Sometimes it was in the barnyard and sometimes it was in the living room. In the winter when grandma couldn't be outside, she was in the living room with a large quilt frame set up near the coal stove where she was making a quilt.

I had a wooden Speedy Flyer wagon and three kittens that I hauled around, even to my grandmother's. I loved going to her house because she had chickens, a cow, a horse and a root cellar dug back into the bank where she kept her garden vegetables that lasted well into the winter. We called it the cave and I remember it being a bit scary because of the spiders that lived in there. She also had a really cool well in the backyard that had a bucket attached by a rope that you lowered into the well to get water. She didn't have water piped into the house. The fun part was letting the bucket fall into the water. I was too little to crank it back up with water in it.

My grandmother Brock was one of the hardest working women that I have ever known. I can remember watching her mow the hayfield with a sythe and when the hay was dry she would rake it up in piles and then tie a rope around the pile and drag it to the barn where she stored it for the animals in the winter. She also had a gardern plot where she raised all the vegetables that she canned in jars each summer for the winter.

She always had a neat looking place. She loved flowers and had them planted everywhere around the house. Her weed wacker was a sickle that she used for weed control. She milked the cow twice a day and made her own butter, some of which she sold. I have kept her butter churn, butter bowl, butter keeper and scales that she used to weigh out the butter that she sold. These are relics that are a connection for me to the past. I often helped her churn the butter by working the plunger up and down. She would also make what she called "smearcase," or cottage cheese. It was like a sour cottage cheese and she made it by scalding the by-product of churning butter or the buttermilk. She took the milk and let it sour in a crock in the kitchen. When the milk curdled, she would put it in a muslin cloth bag to rinse and then let drain. I can still smell it. Not pleasant.

She also raised chickens to sell. They would be what we call today "free range" chickens. They had free range of the back yard. I loved to collect the eggs. The hens had their favorite places to lay the eggs and some were hard to reach, like under the shed. I can remember the chopping block in the back yard. An old stump with two big nails pounded into it side by side and just far enough apart to get a chickens neck into. She would put the chickens neck between the spikes and then with one fell swoop of her hatchet; off would come the head.

Ever heard the metaphore "running around like a chicken with its head cut off?" I've seen it. It is absolutely amazing how far a chicken can run without it's head. The first time I saw it I was absolutely astounded. Later on grandma got wise and would tie their feet and wings together and string them up on the closeline with their heads down and one-by-one cut their heads off with a very sharp butcherknife. Then she would dip the whole chicken into a pot of boiling water to release the feathers. Then came the dirty and smelly job of pluckig the chicken. You pulled off all the wet feathers you could and then all the little fuzz or hair was singed off over an alchol flame. I have plucked more then my share and don't ever care to do it again. Hot wet chicken feathers and singed hair are the worst when it comes to the smell, not to mention that the wet feathers stick to your fingers. What can I say? Nasty!

As I said, I never knew my grandfather Brock. This is a picture of him and my grandmother with their old horse Mac.

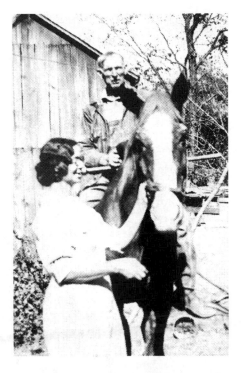

The Big Move

It was a sad day when we sold our little cottage in the hollow to move to Hopewell, more than 10 miles away, to the farm that my dad and mom purchased. That happened in July 1947 and meant that I could no longer walk with my wagon and kittens to my grandmother's house. Dad had always wanted a farm of his own so he purchased 25 acres along the Old National Highway, or the old Route 40, the first national road project of the United States Federal Government.

It reached Zanesville by 1831, and incorporated the Zanes Trace that came through Zanesville, down Main Street and across the Y-Bridge. The Y-Bridge is the only one like it in the world. When people were asking directions, you could actually tell them to go to the center of the bridge and turn right or left. They often looked at you with a puzzled sxpression.

Growing Up Years

That first year on the farm was tough. Dad did a lot of research and talking to neighbors about "how to farm." He was a city boy all his life and now a "wannabe farmer." Our property bordered a farm owed by Jake Davis, who had an apple orchard. He was a big help to dad. Dad would help him with his crops and he would help us with ours. Dad didn't have a lot of money that first year so he went to some auctions and purchased various pieces of used farm equipment that were, to say the least, "well used" and constantly breaking down. We always had something torn down in the barn and dad would work on it when he got home from his real job at the Hazel Atlas Glass plant where he worked six hours a day, seven days a week. Some of the used equipment included a Farmall F-14 steel-wheeled tractor that came

with a mowing machine, a plow, and a harrow for breaking up the ground once plowed. Other stuff included a dump hay rake that I spent a lot of hours sitting on that dad used to rake up the hay so we could haul it into the barn on a flatbed hay wagon. I was able to rescue the seat and one of the wheels off the old hayrake that had been junked at the back of the property years after dad sold the farm. A little more of the clutter that I keep around to remind me of my roots.

Dad used the fall and winter of 1947 to get everything ready for plowing and planting the next spring. I remember the large garden that we planted, the fence we put up for the chickens, the hog pen that dad constructed and later learned that you had to put nearly as much wire fencing under the ground as you had on top of the ground to keep the hogs from routing under the fence and roaming where they pleased. Dad learned a lot of lessons about farming the hard way during our first few years on the farm.

Dad's first hay crop was cut our first year on the farm. We had a large hay fork in the barn so we could pull the loose hay up into the haymow using the tractor. There were also two large trap doors that opened to a shoot and steps where we would throw the hay down to the pen where we kept the cows in winter. In the fall, dad cut the corn by hand and put it into corn shocks. The shocks would stay in the field until we needed them for cattle feed; then we could load them on the flatbed wagon and haul them to the barn where we would would first husk the corn off the stalk and then run them through the corn fodder chopper as feed for the cows.

The barn was definitely a place of a lot of activity. It served as a mechanic shop, storage for hay, a cow pen, milking stations with stanchions that the cows put their heads through and were locked in so we could milk, a horse stall, and of course we had a basketball court with the backboard and rim mounted on the edge of one of haymows.

In 1948 we had a new edition to the family. On October 16 my brother Stephen Allen ("Steve") was born. To help my mom, Grandma Brock moved from her farm in the hollow along Ridge Road and came to live with us permanently until she passed in 1965. She lived with us a total of 17 years. I remember when Steve came home from the hospital he was quite ill with asthma or some kind of breathing difficulty. We had his bassanette in the dining room and grandma would take care of him during the night when he couldn't breathe.

My grandmother Brock was super spiritual but also very superstitious. When Steve was old enough to stand on his own, she had him stand up against the door casing in her bedroom. My dad marked his height and then drilled a hole at that spot. My grandmother cut a lock of hair from the crown of his head and stuffed it into the hole. She closed the hole with a peg of wood and pronounced that whenhe grew above it his asthma would be gone. I don't know if it was her faith in this process or her constant prayer, but when he grew above it the asthma was gone.

I was so excited to have a brother. The only problem was I had already started school that year so during our growing up years we didn't have a lot in common with the exception of both having German measles at the same time and being quarantined with scarlet fever. I was into cowboys and indians and it didn't take Steve long to take an interest as well. One time, some of my cousins were visiting and playing cowboys and indians in the yard. Steve and one of our cousins was playing in the sandbox in the backyard. As a daring move, at an imaginary rescue, I threw my gun to one of my partners who was chasing the indians. Instead, it hit my brother's head that required a visit to the emergency room.

Before we had a TV, I would never miss an episode of The Roy Rogers show on the radio. He was always involved in an action-packed wild west adventure. I guess there were a lot of western shows in the late 1940s and early 1950s that captured my attention. They always ended every episode with Roy Rogers and Dale Evans singing, *Happy Trails to You.*

Grandpa Renicks bought me a horse for my tenth birthday so I was really hot stuff. I think I lived in a bit of a fantasy world at that time. I rode happy trails on my horse named Judy. I rode Judy nearly every week, even in the winter weather permitting and sometimes everday in the summer. I would ride with a saddle or just bareback. I could even ride her without a briddle although she was impossible to control when she decided to head for the barn. I got left hanging on the barn door rail more than once just because I was too tall to fit under the door header when I was on her back. I would ride to the back of the property through the woods and imagine I was a real cowboy. I would also ride to Mt. Sterling to the post office or to the store and would stop to see one of my cousins along the way. Did I mention that I had a rabid imagination?

I saved up my money and bought a Gurnsey heffer from old Wesley Winegartener who lived just down the road when I was 10 years old. He was an old bachelor. I was so proud of her and looked forward to the day she would have calves of her own. However, somehow she got hold of piece of wire fence that she ate and it punctured her stomach and she died. It as a sad day at our house. However, the next spring when the calves were born Mr. Winegartner came one day to let me know that he was giving me another heffer calf to replace her. I ended up with three milk cows and each spring I would sell the calves for veal.

School Years

I started the first grade of school in September of 1948 at the Hopewell Rural School. Classes were small and the school went from first to twelfth grade. My first-grade teacher was Mrs. Irene Starkey. She was a tough teacher and she expected perfection. If she was talking, you had better be paying attention. You didn't dare even fiddle with your pencil or you got cracked across the knuckles with her pointer stick. Would you like to know how I know that? The first two guesses don't count. She did teach us to memorize scripture passages like the 23rd Psalm and the Lord's Prayer.

Her sister-in-law was the third-grade teacher. She was even more severe and stern. Everyone was afraid of her. She had an exceptionally long neck and we used to call her old rubber neck. She did teach me good penmanship and how to write cursive.

I started playing the Cornet by the time I was in second grade. By sixth grade I started playing in the high school band and especially the marching band. I continued with that through all my high school years and by the time I was a senior I joined the musician's union and started playing with the Zanesville Memorial Band. We did concerts in the park on Friday nights under the direction of William Erwine. I actually got paid to play. My high school years were fun years filled with playing various parts in drama productions, music and basketball laced with a few pranks with my high school buddies.

For our senior trip our class boarded an Amtrak train in Newark, Ohio, and rode the rails through Horseshoe Bend to Washington, D. C. We had a great trip, and everyone was on their best behavior because we knew we would be sent home if we weren't. None of us wanted to deal with the consequences of that. We graduated a grand total of 21. I was third from the top in the class. We wrote our own class song and at commencement several of us gave speeches or highlights of our high school years.

Spiritual Heritage

Life for our family changed dramatically in 1953-1954, when I was 11 or 12 years old. I'm not real certain of the date that it started or how long it was before dad finally went to the doctor and found out that he had bleeding stomach ulcers. His heavy smoking wasn't helping, and he was admitted to the hospital to have about two-thirds of his stomach removed. He was in the hospital for an awfully long time. As a result of the many IVs that he had in his arm, a large lump rose on his left forearm. On further investigation, a biopsy showed that it was cancer. He was sent to University Hospital in Columbus, Ohio for surgery. The lump was removed but the cancer returned, and he had to go back for a second surgery. The surgeon told dad before the second surgery that he wasn't sure he could save his arm and that he might have to amputate at the elbow. Dad made a vow to the Lord that if He would save his arm that he would serve him the rest of his life. His arm was spared, but he bore an ugly scar that was a constant reminder of his commitment to the Lord. I remember he got home just before Christmas of 1954.

By the spring of 1955, dad became very pensive. Mom was concerned that he might be going into some sort of post-operative depression. He continued to be very moody until sometime in the summer of '55. What was really going on came to the forefront on a Sunday evening while we were waiting for Uncle Ed and Aunt Mary to pay us a visit like they always did on Sunday evening. Dad appeared in the kitchen dressed in a suit and tie. He announced that he was going to church and if any of us were going with him we needed to be ready in 15 minutes. Needless to say, we were shocked. Steve and I were dirty from playing outside and mom was working in the kitchen making something to eat that evening. We did a lot of quick scrubbing and scrambling to get dressed to go. We had no clue where we were going, only that it was to church somewhere. We didn't know until we arrived. On the way there nobody said a word. Dad continued in his pensive state and everyone was afraid to ask where we were going.

We ended up at the Christian and Missionary Alliance church on Epply Ave. This is the church that my grandmother had helped start. Dad had obviously been doing some reconnaissance to locate the place and the time. I'm sure the tiny congregation was shocked to see a family of four walk in, nearly doubling the number of people present. At the close of the service an invitation was given and amazingly dad sang almost the entire invitation hymn, "Just as I Am," without looking at the words. After the first or second stanza, Dad made a beeline to the front of the church, kneeling at the altar. He wept bitter tears of remorse. He was gloriously saved! I wasn't sure what that meant. This was the beginning of the fulfillment of the vow that he made to the Lord when he was frightened that he would lose his arm in surgery. All I know is he was a different person and from that night on every time the church doors were open, we were there. It was the beginning of a spiritual revolution for our family. We went from being occasional church attenders to being actively engaged and to say the least as a family we were spiritually awakened to a greater purpose.

In January 1956, my freshman year of high school, word came that five missionaries had been martyred in the jungles of Ecuador. My heart was stirred spiritually and that summer I gave my life to Christ in a revival service conducted by an evangelist called Daddy Weston. I held out to the last night and by that time I was so under conviction I was compelled to go forward and give my life to Christ. Church became a focal point of my life. Rev. Don Jacobson, my pastor, mentored me, encouraged me and took me to Susque Boys Camp in the heart of the Bald Eagle Mountain range in north central Pennsylvania along Lycoming Creek. The camp was in Trout Run, just north of Williamsport. I went for three summers in a row and was exposed to a whole new world where my spiritual life was deepened through

Bible study with camp counselors who took a special interest in each one of us throughout the time we were there. My last summer at camp I joined the staff and worked in the kitchen for three weeks.

As my spiritual life deepened, I became more and more interested in going to Bible College. At Beulah Beech Bible Conference on the last Sunday afternoon of the conference in 1959 they had a massive missionary rally with a missionary speaker. At the end of a very stirring service, an invitation was given for those who wanted to come forward to dedicate themselves to missions. The service closed by singing the old hymn O Zion Haste.

> *O Zion Haste thy mission high fulfilling, to tell to all, the world*
> *that God is light, that he who made all nations is not willing,*
> *one soul should parish lost in shades of night.*

Then this verse was the clincher for my mom and dad.

> *Give of thy sons to bear the message glorious, give of thy wealth to speed*
> *them on their way, pour out thy soul for them in prayer victorious, and all thou*
> *spendest Jesus will repay.* Written by, Mary Ann Thompson

Mom and dad went forward with other much younger people who were dedicating themselves to missionary service. Steve and I were totally baffled. They were both too old to be missionaries.

Over a meal after the service, Steve and I asked them what they were doing. Did they think they could be missionaries? They said, "No, but we gave you two to be missionaries. We were responding to the words of the hymn." Woah! What a revelation and prophecy.

College Years 1960-1965

I had been accepted to St. Paul Bible College and Nyack Missionary College. The day we left the farm I still hadn't decided where I was going. If we went west, I would have gone to St. Paul Bible College in St. Paul. Minnesota. If we went east, I would end up at Nyack Missionary College in Nyack, New

York. Dad drove to the end of the driveway as said, "Are we going east or west?" That's when I made my decision for Nyack.

When I decided to go to Nyack, I left behind a steady girlfriend who had been in the youth group and church with me. I think that everyone back home thought that we would eventually marry. I know that she thought that.

As Thanksgiving of my freshman year at Nyack approached, a friend and fellow Ohioan, Tim Evearitt and I decided to hitchhike home because we thought we were homesick. It was a long haul from Nyack to Zanesville and even further for Tim, who lived in Toledo. It took me the better part of 18 hours. When I showed up at the door, I thought my grandmother Brock was going to have a heart attack. Mom was working midnight to eight, so I hid in the bathroom off the kitchen and surprised her when she walked into the kitchen. Once the initial shock wore off, I got the typical mom lecture. What I didn't tell her was that my last ride was with a bunch of drunk guys. As you might imagine, I returned to New York City by Greyhound bus.

By this time, I realized that I had to get serious with God and it seemed that my relationship with my Zanesville girlfriend was a drawback to my faith. Every Friday evening at Nyack we had a missionary meeting with a profoundly serious emphasis on missions and challenges to respond to the Great Commission. One meeting stands out specifically in my mind. The speaker was Helen Constance, who shared the struggle she had with sending her children from Chile to Quito, Ecuador to boarding school at a young age. She had gotten a telegram from the school to say that their son Joe, still in elementary school, was gravely ill. Her only mode of transportation was bus, which would take several days. She confessed that she didn't know if Joe would be alive or dead by the time she arrived. She said something to the effect that she trusted God in the dark of night and believed he was sovereign regardless of the outcome. She also shared the important role that the Alliance Academy was playing in the care and development of her children. That was an event that deepened my commitment to a specific call to missions with a clear direction to be a missionary teacher at the Alliance Academy. This happened early in my sophomore year.

When I went home for Christmas that year, I broke up with "the girlfriend." I believe it was more painful for her than it was for me because I already had my eye on the girl of my dreams. In fact, I told my Aunt Mary that I had found the girl I was going to marry, and this was before the first date. She was a preacher's daughter. That should have scared me away, especially because her dad was a preacher from Western PA. He turned out to be a great guy. I started dating Joyce on February 24, 1962. We had good times together. She loved to do the same things that I did. We loved to ice skate together and loved the outdoors, especially in the spring and summer.

I had a car, a 1955 Chevy Belair, that I had spent the summer overhauling. It was a flathead six and easy to work on. New pistons, rings, rods and everything that the motor needed to run smoothly. I also did a major remake of the interior, including carpet, seat covers and blue running lights. My mom's cousin Bobby Lucas, a mechanic, helped me.

I went to visit Joyce at the end of the school year in 1962 when I had a chance to meet her family. They thought I had to be foreigner because they had never heard a name like Renicks. I could have said the same of them I guess with a name like Armitage. Her brothers and sisters were a trip. The very first time I visited I got the famous "water glass." It was a genuinely nice glass that had been hand cut. The oddity about it was that one of the cut roses on the side of the glass had been cut through so that when you drank from it, it dribbled down your chin and onto your shirt. They thought that was hilarious. I guess this was my test to see if I would fit into their zaney family. Debbie who was only ten years old eventually adopted me as a big brother. She would sit on my lap in the rocking chair.

I was always up for a good prank. Vernon Church had given me a ticket to attend the International Flower Show at Columbus Circle in New York City. On the way with a friend, I noticed that the Queen Mary was in dock. I had him drop me off and I took a tour. While on board, I found the library and purchased a post card with a picture of the Queen Mary. I posted it in a box that would be mailed from Southampton, England. I told my parents of the wonderful opportunity I had to visit England and that I would be home in the summer. When my parents received the post card, my mother was livid and wanted to call the President of Nyack and let him have it. Dad was the levelheaded one and calmed her down. He suggested she call the college and see if I was there.

When I was located by the college switchboard operator, the result was the dressing down of my life. That same day after the flower show I had run out of money for subway fare back to Washington Heights to catch the bus to Nyack. I had my bus ticket so I decided to walk. The farther I went the more the culture changed. I suddenly found myself in the heart of Harlem. Harlem was not the place to be for a white guy. I stopped a policeman who put me on a bus, but when we reached the end of the line, I was across a soccer field and two stories of steps below where I needed to be. This was late at night and I was scared. I was also afraid I would miss the last bus out at 11. I did make it back to Nyack.

I wasn't sure where Joyce stood as far as being a missionary. One late night sitting on the couch in the living room on the farm, I told her that I felt God's call to be a missionary but had been afraid to tell her because I didn't know if she felt the same. There was a huge sigh of relief. This shared commitment deepened our relationship and resolve to follow God's leading and to pursue missionary service.

There was a little Italian pizza joint in Congers, NY, where I first approached the subject of marriage with Joyce. We loved that little hole in the wall, not only for the great pizza, but it was just our special place. The owner was a true Italian and would often come out and sing *O Solo Mio* with the player piano. There were red and white striped awnings along the wall over the booths with paintings of Italy on the wall. There was also a red and white striped awning over the front of the building. It was a very romantic place. We were engaged that December just before going home for Christmas. I drove Joyce to the top of the mountain, and we parked the car overlooking the Tappan Zee Bridge. At night it looked like two strings of pearls across the Hudson River. It was a very romantic spot. We dated for about 18 months and in the meantime got to know each other's families quite well.

The summer before we were married, I was working at Brockway Glass in Zanesville. This was part of our plan to make a bundle of money for our honeymoon and furnishing our apartment back at Nyack. I was working on tank repair where we had to chip large pieces of glass so a brick retaining wall could be rebuilt. I had my hand smashed by a sledgehammer. It cut my hand and had to have multiple stiches. Joyce was there for a bridal shower and I can remember her sitting up all night by my bedside. This should have been a warning to her to run the other way. How many nights since then has she done the same?

III

Beginning Our Lives Together

Our Wedding

WE WERE MARRIED on August 24, 1963, in Butler, Pennsylvania in the Main Street Alliance Church. Our honeymoon was to be a trip to Front Royal, Virginia and the Luray Caverns on to the Skyline Drive. When we left Butler following the reception, Joyce started crying as we drove down Route 8 toward Washington, PA. I wasn't sure how to take that. I didn't know if she decided she had made a mistake and regrated what she had done or what. It turned out they were tears of relief. We had our first night at The Washington Motel in Washington, Pennsylvania.

Our first day we drove to Front Royal, Virginia on our way to the Skyline Drive and the Luray Caverns. We spent our second night in Luray at a cheaper motel (all we could afford), but it had a pool. Unfortunately, I ate something that gave me food poisoning and ended up in the hospital the next morning after heaving my toenails all night long. We went to a local hospital and they thought I might have a burst appendix, but there was no doctor. He was on vacation. They told Joyce that she needed to get me back over the mountains to Front Royal where there was a hospital with a doctor that could treat me or operate or do whatever was needed. They said, don't hurry but don't waste any time. Joyce backed the car up to that little porch and threw our stuff over the rail into the trunk of the car. I know that Joyce was scared to death, but she had just said her vows to stay by my side in sickness and in health to death do us part. I felt like I was going to die.

It's a long story not worth telling all these years later, but it ended up that I had a very compassionate doctor who found Joyce the nicest motel of any place she stayed the whole honeymoon while I had a hospital room. The doctor never billed us for his services and paid for the motel. Joyce's dad was ready to come and rescue his daughter, but she showed what she was made of and told him that she was married now, and she could handle it and handle it she did. What a girl.

Our First Home

We had already put a deposit down on a small two room apartment in Nyack on South Highland Avenue within an easy walk of the college and Vernon Church Flowers where we both had jobs. Joyce was the bookkeeper and I was a floral designer. When it came time to go back to Nyack after I recovered from our honeymoon, our parents helped us load up a U-Haul trailer that we pulled behind our car with some furniture from them and some that we had bought. We were all set and off we went for our senior year at Nyack.

It was a momentous year. In November, our President John F. Kennedy was assassinated. The nation was shocked and in mourning. Joyce and I along with Marshall and Maryann Gilliam and Pam and Lowell Heim crowded into Marshall's car and off we went to Washington D.C. to see the fallen President. The only problem was that the heater didn't work and neither did the defroster. It was a "togetherness" kind of trip. We arrived in Washington in the wee hours of the morning only to find out that we were too late to get in line to go through the rotunda of the Capitol to pay our respects. We had a great time together and are still friends with both couples as of today. Maryann shares an especially important tradition with us as she is an Alabama fan, "Roll Tide".

We loved our little apartment in Nyack. The kitchen was a makeover closet and small. It was a path from the bedroom to the living room. The only drawback was that the bathroom was in the hall outside our bedroom door. It was so tempting to just look out a crack in the door to see if anyone was out there and then dash out in my underwear or sometimes without it. There was an apartment that was a mirror image of ours just across the hall. Their bathroom was at the other end of the hall. One couldn't be too careful, or you might get caught.

In March Joyce got pregnant, which was not part of the plan. She graduated in June. Both of our parents and Aunt Mary and Uncle Ed came to Joyce's gradation. I delayed my graduation so I could take some additional courses that Nyack had added to the History/Social Studies curriculum. This extra work gave me a better major. However, I have always considered the class of 1964 to be my class.

By the end of June 1964, Joyce began to question what was happening with the baby. She stopped feeling life and went to the doctor only to find out that the baby was dead in her womb. We were shocked and deeply saddened. By mid-July Joyce aborted the baby naturally. We don't know what happened and those were different days in the medical profession than they are today. The doctor allowed me to see the baby while Joyce was still sedated. It was a perfectly formed baby boy. When I asked how we were to handle the burial, the hospital informed me that they would take it from here. I guess we were too naive and didn't know to press our rights. To this day, we regret that Joyce didn't get to hold the baby and we didn't get to name him or bury him. Looking back, the hospital didn't give us a choice. This loss still touches a raw nerve whenever we talk about it.

Life goes on. Joyce worked full time at the flower shop, and I worked as near full time as possible, working around my classes. The time at Vernon Church Flowers was another education for me that was like an unofficial degree in floral design. It has proven to be a lifetime skill that I have used frequently. It is something that I really enjoy.

Grandma Ollie Lucas Brock

1964 was a sad year. Grandma Brock went to be with Jesus, whom she loved dearly. Joyce and I drove to Zanesville from Nyack for the funeral on May 25. She was a godly saint who prayed fervently for anyone and everyone in need. I can still see her standing at the kitchen sink at the farmhouse doing dishes praying for someone. Sometimes she would raise her hands and pray in tongues. She lived with us for 17 years and was like a mother to Steve and me. Mom worked shift work at the glass plant, so Grandma Brock was always there to make sure we were taken care of.

Joyce and I enjoyed living in Nyack and exploring the surrounding areas. We were only a 30-minute drive into New York City. There were a lot of things that we enjoyed about New York: the preaching of Dr. Stephen Olford, who pastored the Calvary Baptist Church, concerts at Carnegie Hall, strolls in Central Park, Rockefeller Center at Christmas with all the lights, the big tree and ice skating. Another Christmas tradition for us was the organ and choir concert at Riverside Church located in Upper Manhattan.

Just 30 minutes north of Nyack up 9W toward West Point along the Hudson River was the moth ball fleet of battleships that made it back from WWII. At West Point, it was something to watch a full-dress parade of cadets or listen to a concert in the cadet chapel performed by the West

Point Chorale combined with the Nyack College Chorale singing Handel's Messiah. There were times that we would just take Sunday afternoon and go to West Point to enjoy a walk along the Hudson River or drive around Storm King Mountain in the fall when the leaves had changed.

At Bear Mountain State Park, you could watch ski jumping in winter. There was always the drive down the other side of the Hudson Valley after crossing Bear Mountain Bridge through Sleepy Hollow of Rip Van Winkle fame. Along that drive is the Vanderbilt Mansion, the home place of Franklin D. Roosevelt and his presidential library. This whole drive is so rich in history. Then we would end up in Tarrytown and cross the Tappan Zee Bridge at the widest point in the Hudson River, nearly 3 miles, and we were back in Nyack.

Our Professional Careers in Education

At the end of my senior year in May 1965 we packed up our belongings and moved to Zanesville, Ohio. We rented the first floor of a large two-story house on Brighton Blvd. in Zanesville. Joyce and I both got teaching positions in the West Muskingum school district. Joyce taught third grade at Dillon School and I taught 7th and 8th grade history and geography at Hopewell School. It was strange going back to the same school where I had spent 12 years from 1st to 12th grade. I taught for the same principal, Harlan Foltz, that had been my high school principal. In fact, it was very strange when I started teaching kids whose parents I had gone to school with. I taught at Hopewell for 7 years before being asked to take a teaching principalship at Richey Elementary School. I taught 5th and 6th grade social studies and was the administrator.

While Joyce was teaching at Dillon/Richey Schools, she got pregnant. Since she had lost our first child, we were scared. Joyce's doctor told her to eat lots of oranges. So instead of kids bringing the teacher apples, they brought her oranges. They kept her supplied, so we didn't have to buy them.

Beginning the Family Adventure

Our first child was a boy, Marshall Jerome, born on November 9, 1966. He had a very orange complexion when he was born. Must have been all those oranges. We had moved from Brighton Boulevard to a small house on a hill near Hopewell school before Marshall was born. The little yellow house had a history. There was still a bullet hole in the kitchen wall where the Sheriff had shot at the man who lived there in the process of an arrest for a domestic dispute. Marshall was the first grandchild in both families. Joyce's mom came to help take care of him.

We had a great garden with lots of tomatoes, pumpkins, cucumbers and a host of other vegetables. We did a lot of canning, made dill pickles, bread and butter pickles and sauerkraut.

Just 14 months later, along came Melissa Joyce, born on January 15, 1968. We had more than 20 inches of snow on the ground and even though we had gone into town to stay at my parents to be closer to the hospital, it was an exceedingly difficult trip to the hospital. By the time I got Joyce there, the nurses took her up to a room immediately and got her settled. I had to check her in and by the time I got upstairs she had already given birth. From the time we arrived until the time Melissa was born it was only15 minutes. She wasn't waiting for anybody. I walked into the waiting room about the time the nurse came out and called my name to announce that I had a daughter. One guy said, "That's not fair, I've been here for hours." There was great excitement in the Renicks family because she was the first girl in our family.

Marshall was too laid back to walk so we were carrying two babies. We were concerned that something was wrong, but Dr. Elliot said, "Don't worry he'll walk when he's ready." He was learning to talk, and talk he did, but I guess he couldn't walk and talk at the same time.

We had a bit of a breather – 21 months – before Michaela Jean came along. Michaela was born on October 11, 1969. We were totally pumped to get another girl. We didn't have a car when it was time to take Joyce to the hospital. I had been to the hospital to visit my dad who had pneumonia and on the way home on Old Falls Road a thousand-pound bull came off an embankment on a curve right in front of the car. The car was totaled and had an indentation of the bull in the grill. After some frantic scrambling, mom and dad loaned us one of their cars. They brought it to us in exchange for Marshall and Melissa.

Now we had three under the age of three. What a handful. Michaela gave us a scare when she was five months old. She was hospitalized with what they called "the fifth disease." I can still see the IV needle in a vein in her forehead.

Marshall also gave us a scare. He was in a walker buzzing around the kitchen while Joyce was getting supper. She was frying porkchops in an electric skillet and he proceeded to grab the cord and pull the skillet down on top of his head. The grease ran down his arm and burned him badly. God was faithfully protecting him because none of the hot grease got on his face. His arm scarred quite badly.

The kids had a fenced in yard, with a wading pool and a beautiful Dalmatian dog named Dodie.

More Educational Opportunities

It was during my three years at Richey Elementary School that I was working on my Masters' degree at Xavier University in Cincinnati, Ohio. These were stressful times. After working all week, I would get up a 4am on Saturday morning and drive three hours for a couple of classes and then drive back. During the summer, I would go down and spend the week and come home on weekends. One of my classmates was legally blind and couldn't see to type his papers so I typed them in exchange for third base box seats at Cincinnati Reds baseball games and he also paid me per page. This was during the days of the "Big Red Machine" of the 1970s, when the Reds won two World Series titles.

This time of busyness put a lot of stress on the family and especially Joyce with the responsibility of three kids and being pregnant again. In 1973 we borrowed a friend's tent top camper and drove to Erlanger, Kentucky, where spent the week in a KOA campground. What a trip that was, all five of us in that small camper, right beside the railroad tracks. I was driving into Xavier every day for classes; I had a bad case of the gout in my foot and was on crutches, trying to keep up with all the kids' activities. Did I mention that Joyce was pregnant? This week was one of those "family togetherness" times that was priceless. Try setting up a tent camper on crutches. Very tricky! On one of my light days for classes we took the kids to Cincinnati Zoo.

Getting my master's degree was hard work and demanding for the whole family, but in the end, it paid off. During my last year at Richey School, I was asked to give part of my time to the West Muskingum Schools central office to work on the design, program, and hiring of teachers for the new middle school that was to open the fall of 1974. All indications were that I was to assume the principalship of the new middle school. I was excited about it because it was one of the open school concepts that seemed to be the fad at the time.

While I was busy at Richey School as its teaching principal, Joyce had been working with the pastor and elders of the Alliance Church considering the concept of a preschool. She worked at developing the curriculum, equipping a large empty room at the church and finding a teacher helper in Evelyn Stires, my cousin. In my summer spare time, I researched and built the furniture for the preschool. Faye and Rue Wittlinger contributed financially and provided moral support. It became Wee Pals Nursery School. It started small and grew rapidly by word of mouth. Joyce continued as director until we went to Ecuador, when she turned it over to Susan Ryder.

After the church moved to Richey Road, the church sold it to an outside entity. On September 27, 1973, Matthew Joel was born. It was a beautiful fall day. By the time the fourth one came along we had the routine down. Joyce was induced and we were all anxious for the baby to be born. I had a meeting to go to and it seemed like he would never come. We were thrilled with another boy. We had bought a house in 1970 on Ridge Road, but with four kids it seemed rather small. Marshall was excited to have a baby brother to share his room, but with the crib it was small. He was a good baby and had to go with the flow of a busy household. He attended his first evangelistic crusade when he was four months old.

IV

Challenges and Decisions

Key '73

DURING THE EARLY part of 1973 I was contacted by one of the pastors in Zanesville who was also the President of the Parent and Teachers Association at Richey School. He asked if I would head up a Zanesville chapter of a national movement of evangelism for the city called Key '73. At first, I turned him down thinking that I couldn't add one more thing to what I was already doing. He was very persuasive, though, and I agreed to go to an organizational meeting with him. I was asked to make a presentation of what I would do if chosen for the position. There was also a presentation before mine by a Catholic gentleman. I had told the pastor who invited me that I would only consider it if I received a unanimous vote. After my presentation, all the Catholics walked out and when the vote was taken, it was unanimous.

There was an organizing committee to form, meetings to be held, door-to-door canvasing to coordinate and regular noontime prayer vigils in churches and empty store fronts across the city. Church bells would toll the hour for prayer and people would stop and pray. That year culminated in a weeklong citywide evangelist campaign in January 1974. The crusade was put on by the Ford Philpot Evangelistic Team and held in the Municipal Auditorium. We had gotten well acquainted with the Team because they came throughout the year to work in planning and preaching in the participating churches in the community. This was all part of the promotion for the crusade. On one Sunday morning in a Lutheran church several people went forward at the end of the service to receive Christ, including the pastor. The Crusade was a huge success with hundreds in attendance each night and decisions for Christ every service.

The last night of the crusade I had the privilege of counseling one of my former students from Hopewell. Rose Ihinger gave her heart to Jesus that evening and that began a new relationship for our family. Rose was in foster care and living at the Children's Home. We had her come to our home for the weekends, which gave us the opportunity to get to know her better and hopefully provide the discipleship that would help her develop in her faith. She had a million questions and many nights we would sit up late trying to help her find the answers to some of the deep soul troubling issues that she had about God. This was the last semester of her senior year. She had been less than a stellar student, but as the semester progressed, she changed. Her faith in Jesus had made a huge difference in her attitude. Joyce and I attended her graduation and when the awards were given, she received the award for the most improved student for the year and had done it in one semester. We were so proud of her.

After graduation, Rose had to leave the Children's Home because she had aged out of the foster care system. She packed all her belongings in one cardboard box and came to live with us. I remember one time that she decided to cook for the family. She was going to bake a whole chicken. She laid it on it back on the counter and started pumping its legs to give it some exercise because she thought it looked scrawny. She was very squeamish about putting her hand inside the chicken. *"You mean I have to stick my hand in there to take that stuff out?"* We had many good times together and Rose became like a daughter to us and a big sister to the kids.

Life Altering Decisions

One of the members of the advance team for the Philpot Association was Willis Braun, a former Alliance missionary to the Congo. We had a special affinity for him in that we were both from Alliance roots. As we were taking him back to his hotel the final night of the crusade, he said to Joyce and me, "So what are you going to do now?" That was a bit of a surprise because I planned to go on and be the principal of the new middle school, although I still didn't have a contract and I had been issuing contracts to all the new teachers. He said, "Surely you can't go back to being a principal." He then told us about the country of Liberia and the fact that he knew the President of the country personally. The President was asking that he send someone who could help develop, with the pastors of Liberia, a national movement of evangelism. Willis thought that with the experience and success of the crusade in Zanesville, I was well suited to do that. Joyce and I prayed earnestly about it and felt God's leading in this direction. I received a letter from the President of Liberia, Dr. William Tolbert, asking that I come and teach in the Education Department of the University of Monrovia while leading the evangelism movement. We had asked Joyce's dad if he could tell us how we could be sure that this was the will of God. He replied, *"All I can say is that you have to know in your heart that this is what God wants, because when the hard times come you can take God back to that place and say, 'we're here Lord because we know you want us here and you will see us through."*

About the middle of March, I went to the West Muskingum Superintendent's office and tendered my letter of resignation as Principal at Richey School. The Superintendent was flabbergasted, but I reminded him that I hadn't been issued a contract for the Middle School position. He started backpedaling and said he would postdate the contract and that I couldn't resign because he was counting on me for the position of principal. When I said I was sorry, but we were confident of God's calling on our lives for this new opportunity, he looked at me like I had two heads. He didn't understand anything about faith or calling or about God for that matter. My resignation was effective at the end of that school year (1974) and the direction for Africa was set.

What followed is an exceedingly long story so let me try and abbreviate. We were hired by the Ford Philpot Association. We began buying clothes and shoes for the kids for four years and packed all our belongings that we thought we would need in 55-gallon steel drums; we rented our house and moved into the basement of my mom and dads. With our sights set for Africa and the letter of invitation in hand from Dr. Tolbert, we waited and waited and waited. It seemed that all communication with the President's office had broken down.

It was now October and the Philpot Association decided to move forward and bought me a plane ticket on Pan Am for Monrovia through New York, where I had to present myself at the Liberian Embassy for a visa. It was a harrowing experience. I had to call the embassy for an appointment, so I used a pay phone in the lobby of a bank in New York City near the embassy. When I got to the embassy for my appointment, I didn't have my passport. Oh no!! Now what should I do? I began to retrace my steps looking diligently trying to find it. I went back to the bank and looked in the phone booth. Nothing! I went into the bank and asked if anyone had turned it in. With great relief, they handed me my passport. Thank God for big miracles, He proved his faithfulness once again and was just the beginning of his looking out for me! Back to the Embassy for my visa and suddenly I was on my way to Liberia.

When I arrived in Monrovia, I went to the State House and met the President's personal secretary, who informed me that President Tolbert was in New York at an emergency meeting of the UN. He informed me that a new law had been passed eliminating all expats from teaching at the University and that he didn't see any way they could help with my support. Part of my support was to come from my teaching position at the University. What now? My return flight wasn't for 21 days so I decided to make the best of it. I began walking the streets and back alleys of Monrovia, finding little churches and meeting with pastors and missionaries. I decided to make it a fact-finding mission to see if there was interest in a national movement of evangelism. I held a couple of prayer breakfasts sponsored by a missionary, Brian Bliss, at ELWA. Eternal Love Winning Africa (ELWA) was founded in 1953 as Africa's first Christian radio station. We prayed that God would work in the hearts of these pastors and accomplish his purpose. There was indeed a need and it happened without me.

I had a couple of extra days, so I hired a taxi to take me up country to visit a missionary couple from Zanesville who worked at the Phoebe Hospital where I had Liberian Thanksgiving. There was no air conditioning in the taxi, so by the time I arrived I was covered in red dust from the dirt roads. I was told that when you are covered in red dust, you will surely come back to Africa. It was quite evident that God had closed this door to Liberia for us. Interestingly, I had managed to secure visas for the whole family on the strength of the letter from Dr. Tolbert.

Now what Lord?! We're ready to go, ready to serve, but where? We had always hoped we could go to Ecuador and had applied to the C&MA, but they turned us down because we had four kids. Bummer!! I continued to work for the Philpot Evangelistic Association. They rented a large old farmhouse for us in Hopewell. We moved in with a lot of borrowed furniture. We enrolled the kids at Hopewell school, which is ironic in that I went to the same school for 12 years and graduated from there and had taught there for seven years. Money was tight, but God was good to provide people who helped us. I realized quickly that the work I was doing for the Philpot Association was not for me. I also knew that it wasn't benefiting the Association in the way they had hoped.

In early January 1975, Marshall and I made a trip to Lexington, Kentucky to meet with Ford Philpot and Willis Braun to discuss next steps. There wasn't really a clear direction and, on the way home, I decided that it was time to resign and see what God had for us.

And the Phone Rang

By January 1975 we were getting desperate for answers and jobs. Joyce was at a district women's meeting at the Zanesville Alliance Church and I was home with the kids on a snowy day. School was cancelled. Just after lunch 'the phone rang'. It was Arnie Sharesky from the C&MA headquarters in Nyack calling to see if I would be interested in the high school principal's position at the Alliance Academy in Quito, Ecuador. This was a jolt out of the blue. That is where we had wanted to go in the first place. He asked if we could come to Nyack for an interview. Our applications from before were still on file. I gave him a tentative yes but said I would have to talk to Joyce when she returned home, and I would call him. This was an urgent matter for them because of the short amount of time to process us for Quito and have us there by July.

We loaded the kids up and dropped them off with Joyce's mom and dad in Butler, Pennsylvania. The drive to Nyack in January was a snowy, slippery, icy drive, not to mention the cold. What a trip. We were interviewed and interrogated by Arnie Sharesky, L.L. King and David Volstad. We were grilled on everything from our theology to our marriage and family dynamics. When the meeting ended, we went back to Butler and Ohio with the knowledge that we met all the requirements BUT would have to wait for the final decision from the Board of Managers when they met in April. If we were approved by the board, our term of service wouldn't begin until July 1st and then we would start receiving our allowance. On the long drive home, we realized that we had no way of supporting the family or of paying the rent on the farmhouse. Once again we were asking ourselves, what now Lord?

When we got home as we were unloading the car, and 'THE PHONE RANG' again! It was a call from a kindergarten teacher from Richey School asking Joyce to sub for her for 6-8 weeks while she had surgery. The next day, Joyce had to go to the Muskingum County Schools office to fill out the paperwork for the position. She talked with Mr. Murdock, the Superintendent, to see if there were any jobs available for me. Being the middle of the year there were no openings. Joyce was hired to take the kindergarten teacher's place and could start immediately. That was the first big answer to prayer.

By the time she reached Richey school from the County Office, about a 30-minute drive, to talk with the teacher she was replacing, there had been a call from the County Superintendent's office for Joyce. The County Office had just received word from a Principal at the Philo Elementary School that a teacher would be taking sick leave for the remainder of the year and if I was willing to teach 5th grade the job was mine. Two answers to prayer in the space of an hour. Indeed, we serve an awesome God. Both of these jobs lasted until the end of the school year and provided us with the money we needed to live in the big two-story farmhouse in Hopewell. Why were we worrying about the future? A plaque hung in the dining room that read, "The will of God will never lead you where the grace of God cannot keep you."

Packing and Departure for Ecuador

By April, the C&MA Board of Managers had approved us for Quito and then began the mad scramble. We had to be ready to leave by the first part of July and we had much to do. Remember, we were all packed for the hot temperatures of Africa, so what ensued was a frenzy of opening and

unpacking all the steel drums. We had a garage sale of the things we couldn't take to Ecuador. Packing for Ecuador was a whole different experience. We could take things that we wouldn't have thought of taking to Africa. We crated a washer and dryer, a piano and all our earthly possessions in plywood. We also repacked some of the barrels. Ecuador required a different wardrobe for everybody, so shopping became our most frequent pastime. A week before the shipment was to leave Ohio for Ecuador, we got word that the Director of the Academy, Bob Trempert, wanted Joyce to bring everything she would need to start a kindergarten. This was a first for the Academy. She went shopping and I built another crate to hold it all. And we filled it.

The first Sunday of July we had a commissioning service with Rev. Charles Dutt and Joyce's dad at the Zanesville C&MA church. On July 10th we boarded our flight from Columbus, Ohio, to Miami, Florida. My mom and dad, Rose, Joyce's mom and dad, Faye, Rue and Vicki Wittlinger and Rev. and Mrs. Dutt were there to see us off. It was hard to say goodbye. There were a lot of tears. We had said our goodbyes to Rose and we were thankful that she was going to be living with my mom and dad.

Our flight on Ecuatoriana Airlines didn't leave Miami until 3am the next morning. As we were flying across Cuba, the pilot came on the intercom and asked us all to open the shades at our windows and turn on all the lights. The Cubans were showing their muscle by scrambling two MiG fighter jets to escort us through Cuban airspace, one on each wing. That got us all awake when we really wanted to be sleeping.

V

Ecuador

Arrival in Quito

WHEN WE LANDED in the bright sunshine of Quito, we had to deplane and walk across the tarmac. It was then we realized what a colorful plane we had been flying. We had an enthusiastic welcoming committee that included Bob and Marilyn Trempert (Director of the Academy), Marj Sproxton (Elementary Principal), Ruthie Fredrick, Pat and Milton Brown and there may have been others. We learned that we were to stay with the Tremperts until our house was ready. Matthew wouldn't go to anybody or let anyone hold him but Joyce or me. Marshall was thrilled he could go barefoot. His feet got black from the new floor wax and dust and dirt. Bob tried to convince him that it was "jungle rot." A bit later we missed Marshall and found him upstairs in the bathtub scrubbing his feet trying to get rid of the "jungle rot."

The Tremperts were gracious hosts. They took us around Quito to show us the sites and give us an orientation to the neighborhood where we were going to live. We stayed with them for two weeks. They enjoyed taking us to get ice cream cones. During this time, Joyce was busy getting things ready for kindergarten. Joyce inherited furniture from the English Fellowship Church preschool.

I was busy helping Bob Trempert work on the scheduling of high school classes for the opening of school. What a nightmare. All the time I was working on it, I kept saying to myself there must be a better way. We had a huge board on their dining room table that had the eight periods of the day down the side and the classes across the top. We would move little pieces of paper around trying to figure out the fewest conflicts for students and the classes they needed.

They took us furniture shopping and we got the basics to furnish our house. This was all before our shipment arrived, so it was a little like camping out. We didn't have a car or driver's license for Ecuador, so we either had to depend on others for transportation or walk. We did a lot of walking.

We attended some of the Alliance field prayer meetings. We went as families, so the kids got to know several of the other missionary kids. By the time school started, they had made friends and the transition was a little easier. We were invited out by several of the missionary families for meals and we felt really welcome.

The Alliance Academy

This was my first time as a high school principal. I quickly learned that high schoolers were a bit different from fifth graders. I was nervous for the opening assembly of school. All the students grades 7-12, about 250, reported to the gym. I had been told that the previous principal had ruled with an iron fist, didn't trust the kids and was the consummate detective, pulling locker checks or checking lockers after the students had left campus. I decided on a different approach. I reminded the students at the very beginning that I didn't know any of them, and they didn't know me, but as far as I was concerned, we were all starting out with a clean slate. I trusted them unless they gave me reason not to trust them and if they broke the trust, it would be difficult to repair it. This approach seemed to work, and we got off to a great school year.

Shortly after school started, I ended up in Vozandes, the mission hospital, run by HCJB, Herlding Christ Jesus Blessings, "The Voice of the Andes", was the first radio station with daily programming in Ecuador and the first Christian missionary radio station in the world. The station was founded in 1931. I had a serious urinary tract infection, the first of many that year. During the time I was in the hospital, the Tremperts were providing transportation for Joyce and the kids so they didn't have to walk to school. The streets were treacherous to cross. One morning on their way to pick up Joyce and the kids, the Tremperts were involved in an automobile accident that nearly took the life of one of the occupants in the other car. Bob ended up in the transtito jail. Because of the laws in Ecuador, the person at fault was jailed. Even though Bob was not at fault, the woman whose life was hanging in the balance at Vozandes Hospital was the sister of a high ranking Ecuadorian General. Bob was in jail for six weeks, no meals provided and nothing to sleep on but the cold concrete floor. Everyone chipped in to provide Bob with meals. There were more prisoners in his cell than beds, so he had some of the extra mattresses from the dorm brought to the jail for his cell mates to sleep on.

These were unsettled weeks for the school. In Ecuador there was the concept of revenge killing. Because the lady from the accident was near death, the Tremperts were threatened and had to go into hiding with a family who lived in the valley. I was able to return to school after several days and Marj Sproxton and I basically ran the school in Bob's place. As an answer to many prayers, the lady lived, but the school paid dearly.

Health Issues

During the coming months I continued to battle with urinary tract infections. I finally found a doctor in Quito who was able to clearly diagnose the problem as a congenital one that needed surgery but couldn't be done in Quito. In God's providence, one of my nurses at the hospital had worked for a doctor in Miami who specialized in such cases. Yet one more place where God showed His faithfulness. She contacted the doctor and got me an appointment. I flew to Miami courtesy of the C&MA. Through a series of tests, he confirmed what the doctor in Quito had suspected and suggested I needed to return after school finished for surgery.

At about that same time, we had begun noticing that Matthew was very badly bowlegged and walked with his feet turned in. We consulted a doctor in Quito who we found out later suggested the wrong kind of treatment. When I went to Miami for my appointment I also met with a specialist for Matthew. I had his x-rays and the recommendation from the doctor in Quito. The doctor in Miami suggested that the diagnosis for Matthew was wrong according to what he saw on the x-rays. I had met Jack and Sylvia Edwards from the Alliance Church who had recommended the doctor.

Joyce and Matthew flew from Quito and I took them to meet the doctor. He diagnosed the problem and sent us to a brace maker. The first quote on the cost of the brace was far beyond what we could pay: $400+. I asked if there was ever the opportunity to get a used brace. He hesitated and then took a used one off the wall behind him and had us stand Matthew on the counter. He held up the brace and said, "I think I can make this fit." We bought shoes to go on the brace and within 24 hours Matthew was fitted with a brace that turned his feet out at a 45-degree angle. The final cost was $60 plus the shoes that were attached to the brace. We asked how long it would take Matthew to adjust to them. He said once he realizes he can bend and run. That was about an hour. We never did get a bill from the doctor. What an answer to prayer for both Matthew and us! God is faithful.

Joyce wanted to be there for my surgery in July and Matthew needed a follow-up appointment. This was a difficult time for the other three kids because they didn't want to stay in Quito without us and it was a concern for us. So as a family we began praying about it BUT said nothing to anyone. If God didn't provide, then they would have to stay in Quito while were went to Miami. Each week we would find envelopes of money in our mailbox that said for the kid's trip to Miami. We never did know who gave it, but God directed it. Enough money came in to buy tickets for them. Isn't that just like our FAITHFUL God? Joyce, Matthew and my tickets were paid for by the mission. This provision was a gigantic answer to prayer and a great faith builder for the kids. I was scheduled for surgery in early July and I celebrated the bicentennial of the United States on July 4, 1976, in Jackson Memorial Hospital in Miami.

As we started this journey, our parents were a huge support. Phil's parents had come down to spend Christmas 1975 and stayed the month of January.

So, while we were in Miami on the first trip, they stayed with the kids. Joyce's parents came down in June 1976. Dad Armitage was there to speak at the C&MA field conference. While they were there, he had heart issues, probably due to the altitude, and had to leave early. Joyce and the kids flew to Pittsburgh with them so she could see them home safely. Later, I flew to Miami with a contact for a place to stay and a car. This was a Wycliffe couple who made a home available for missionaries who needed to be in the area. I saw the surgeon and had all my pre-op tests. It was a major surgery. As soon as I got to Miami, Joyce, the kids and her mom and dad flew to be with me.

The house we were staying in was old and a bit run down, no air conditioning in the summer heat of Florida, plenty of cockroaches and in the heart of little Havana near the Orange Bowl. Since all the neighbors spoke Spanish, we felt right at home. There were frequent fights among neighbors. People from the Central Alliance Church were horrified when they learned where we were staying. Jack and Sylvia Edwards from the church were a great help and they became great friends. Every time we came through Miami, we planned to stay with them. They were a godly couple who were always encouraging. They were like family.

My surgery was a success. We were supposed to stay in Miami where the doctor could monitor me for six weeks. The only way we could get cool was to go to a mall and sit or walk around. However, because of the heat in Miami and no air conditioning in the house, the doctor let us go back to Ecuador early. Joyce's sister Debbie went with us. The only condition was that I couldn't drive. Since I couldn't drive, some of our friends were good about taking Debbie around to see all the normal tourist sites. Joyce learned to drive a stick shift in Quito traffic.

Furloughs

Our next time home was in 1977 for summer furlough. I had a follow-up with my surgeon. This was a time of traveling to various C&MA churches who had adopted our kids through their women's ministry. We spoke and shared our slide presentation, "Patterns of Ecuador." We also had the kids dress up in Otavalo Indian costumes. I think it scared them for life.

In the summer of 1979, we began our second summer furlough in Butler, Pennsylvania. We furloughed for nine weeks every other year. We had only been home for 10 days when Joyce's dad had a massive heart attack and passed away. Joyce, her mom and sisters were at a women's conference in Slippery Rock, Pennsylvania and Evelyn Christensen was the speaker. It was especially hard on our family because Joyce's dad was to baptize the kids on that coming Sunday. He was preparing for a wedding on Saturday and one of the elders came into his study and asked for the plan for the setup of the church. He reached for his middle desk drawer, laid his head back on his desk chair and took his next breath in heaven.

There was a huge outpouring of love on the part of the church family and the Butler community. People came in droves to the viewing and funeral. Many said, "I didn't attend his church, but he was my pastor." The family was overwhelmed. He was buried in the East Branch cemetery on the road where the first church he pastored once stood, between Spring Creek and Titusville. He is buried next to his daughter Carol. The remainder of our furlough time home was family time along with speaking in churches in Ohio and Pennsylvania.

Living in Ecuador

We lived in the borough of Jippi Joppa in a two-story duplex surrounded by high walls and steel fencing with steel bars on all the windows and doors. At first, it had the feel of a prison but we gradually got used to it. This residence was near the Bull Ring where they had bull fights each year on December 6. Joyce and I went to the bull fights and witnessed some of the most unique pageantry we had ever seen. In Ecuador, the Matador kills the bull over the roar of the crowd. Sometime later we took the whole family. It is a very dressy occasion, somewhat like the Kentucky Derby.

We had some great times in and around Quito. We did a lot of picnics with the Trempert family. One of the most memorable ones was to Cotopaxi. We planned to cook hamburgers, but Marilyn forgot the skillet. What to do? All we had was a shovel that the Tremperts used to clean up their dog's mess in the backyard. So, we took it to the creek and scrubbed it with coarse sand. By this time, it had started to sleet, so we put all 10 of us and the propane stove in the Chevy Suburban and started cooking hamburgers on the shovel after sterilizing it with the heat. Best hamburgers we ever ate.

One of our first major trips outside the city was to Otavalo with Ron and Lorna Tonack, missionary colleagues. They had taken us under their wings and introduced us to Ecuador. Going to and from Otavalo, we crossed over the equator at Cayambe, from the southern hemisphere to the northern hemisphere. The kids bought ponchos with money they had saved. We covered everything in the back of the car while we explored. However, when we got home, we discovered that someone had stolen the ponchos from the

car. A huge disappointment and a lesson learned.

We had many opportunities to travel to Otavalo. We saw some amazing sights, such as Lake Cuicocha, a crater lake high in the Andes Mountains. They say that no one has ever found the bottom. We loved to stroll along the streets of Cotocachi, a town known for its leather goods. It was amazing just to walk in and out of shops and smell the new leather. From there we would travel to the hacienda Chorlavi for lunch. There was always live music and dancing by Otavalo Indians. If you were brave and not faint of heart, you could order a roasted guinea pig on a stick.

One time we were at the hacienda for Joyce's birthday dinner and Matthew requested they play happy birthday. As the instruments played, Matthew was so excited and said, "wasn't it nice that they played it in English mom?" How we laughed at that. From there we would take a short trip across the road to the village of San Antonio de Ibarra home to Ecuador's famous wood carvers. We were able to purchase some amazing wood art from time to time. It was fascinating to stroll from shop to shop watching the actual carvers at work. One of them whom we bought a piece from was famous for carving the doors of the national cathedral in Washington, D.C.

Probably our favorite place was Otavalo, the world's largest poncho market. It is a riot of colors and variety of styles. Everyone is trying to sell you their wares resulting in a cacophony of sounds. The dress of the Otavalo indigenous people is colorful and distinct. One of our favorite Saturday excursions to Otavalo included lunch at Hotel Otavalo where we were treated to great food and the music of the traditional Otavaloan panpipes. This hotel was run by Marge Endra. Marge had been an Alliance Missionary who married an Ecuadorian doctor. The hotel had been his childhood home. Marge also ran the snack bar at the Alliance Academy. She was Matthew's pre-school teacher. Otavalo was the inspiration for our missionary slide presentation "Patterns of Ecuador." There were patterns everywhere, from the cobblestones in the streets to the woven goods to the wooden doors and iron work on homes.

The other place we visited on several occasions was the mission station Agato at the base of Imbabura volcano. This was about five miles east of Otavalo and is known for its woven textiles made on backstrap and Spanish looms. The mountain has an interesting feature in that there is a large indentation in the mountain in the shape of a heart. The Agato C&MA mission station was at the base of the heart and was run by an Alliance single missionary Evelyn Richner. It was an exceedingly difficult and lonely place to serve, and she had only seen one convert in 20+ years.

The people who lived in the area were very violent, especially when they got drunk. It was not uncommon to see men and sometimes women passed out along the narrow cobblestone road that went from the main highway to the mission station with a child or a spouse standing over them to keep their poncho and other valuables from being stolen. Interestingly, the men got drunk on Friday night and the women on Saturday night. However, on the bright side, there had been a breakthrough for the gospel. We were there for the presentation of the first copies of the Quichua New Testament and baptismal service.

On the way home we would often stop in the village of Calderon just outside of Quito where they did Masapán sculpting. This kind of sculpting is a special art form where beautiful and detailed figurines are created from a bread dough mixture. Many of our purchases from nearly 50 years ago still hang on our Christmas tree each year. We always tried to be back in Quito before dark and would end up at the Embajador (blue) Hotel for a piping hot bowl of mushroom soup.

Beach Trips and Mishaps

Another of our favorite trips was to the beach. There were a lot of beautiful beaches in Ecuador. One of the first beaches we visited and returned to several times was Bahia de Caracas with wide hard sand that you could drive on. I made a visit to a doctor for gout and he used a metal tongue depressor that he pulled off the shelf as part of my examination. The patient before me must have had the hiccups because I got a major case of them after getting checked. We stayed the first night in Bahia. In order to get to the beach, we had to cross the bay on a ferry that was made from an old WWII landing craft. It always gave me the willies because it rocked and lurched when I would drive the car, a Chevy Suburban, on to it. This was our first introduction to the Pacific Ocean. We always had to time our trip across the bay when the tide was in. One time we were driving on the beach and came to a place where a small creek was flowing into the bay. A jeep had crossed it just before us so I thought, that's a piece of cake, so I gunned it and the front wheels dropped in and we got stuck. The sand was slowly washing out from under our tires and we were sinking. We were not in four-wheel drive and at the time and you had to change it on the front wheel hubs. Marshall got out and changed it to four wheel and we climbed out of the rut. Did I mention that the car was nearly new and belonged to the school? That was definitely a close call. Our FAITHFUL God was watching over us.

One of our fancy beach trips was to Salinas, an upscale resort. It was just our family and we stayed in a condo owned by a friend from the Batan Alliance Church. This area was a beach where they brought in the giant sword and sail fish. Marshall got the bright idea to take one of the deep-sea fishing poles from the condo and go down to where they had a sword fish strung up weighing it. He stood by the fish with the pole and I took his picture. He showed the picture to his friends at school and they all thought that he had caught it.

Probably the most popular beach was Atacames. We had lots of experiences. One trip was with Marty and Sharon Erickson. We stopped in Santo Domingo de los Colorados to get a stalk of bananas on our way to Esmeraldas and then on to Atacames. This time was a tent camping experience on the beach. There was an Erickson tent and a Renicks tent, with a tarp-covered breezeway in between that served as our kitchen. We strung hammocks between palm trees and hung our big stalk of bananas. What an ideal setting. The rolling tide rocked us to sleep at night after a beautiful Pacific Ocean sunset ushered in the cool of the evening. We all had a super time jumping the surf and flying kites.

On the return trip up through the mountains, our cars got separated in Santo Domingo. As we rounded one of the corners slowly creeping up the mountain toward Quito, we came upon the Erickson's car that had been involved in a horrific accident. They had all been taken to Vozandes Hospital in Quito. We didn't know if they were dead or alive. There was no way to contact anyone! The motor of the pickup that hit them head on and the motor of the Erickson car were jammed together, the windshield had been smashed by somebody's head. A stranger who had stopped to help stayed with the Erickson's car to keep it from being pilfered, while we went back to Santo Domingo to see if we could find the driver of the truck. The Moore's, a missionary family in town, helped us search the morgue, the hospital and all the various clinics. Someone had loaded the driver in the back of another pickup and headed in the direction of Santo Domingo. He was never heard from or seen again. The Erickson's had a long recovery in the hospital. That trip home turned out to be a nightmare.

On yet another trip to Atacames, it was just Marty, his three kids and me along with Marshall and Matthew. Joyce and the girls were in the U.S. for Debbie's wedding. There was only one way in and out of Atacames and it was a narrow two-lane road. Along the road close to the cut off to Quito was Ecuador's only oil refinery. Marty's wife Sharon was flying in from England and he wanted to meet her at the airport. When we got to the refinery the road was blocked with a group of about 100 Ecuadorian soldiers in perfect formation. Marty spoke the best Spanish, so he got out of the car to talk with them. We learned that someone was in the refinery threatening to blow it up. The soldiers were trying to diffuse the situation. We stayed around for a while, gave them cold drinks and they let our kids wear their helmets, hold their tear gas canisters and grenades. After a space of about an hour in the hot sun we decided to go back and enjoy the beach. We made one more attempt to go back to Quito later that afternoon, but this time it was a different group of soldiers who were not as friendly. The leader broke rank and came to the driver's side of the car. He laid his AK-47 in the window and very forcefully told me to turn around and go back. We said, "gracias" and returned to the beach for another night. Trips in Ecuador were never without adventure. I suppose our kids would say no trip with their dad was ever without adventure.

Jungle Trips

One of our other favorite vacation spots as a family was Tena and especially the home of Jerry and Carol Conn. They were like grandparents to our kids. They were at the mission station called Dos Rios. It was a big two-story house that Jerry had built. To get to the house we had to drive across a swinging suspension bridge. The first time I tried it with our Suburban I dropped one of the front wheels through a board that was evidently in need of replacing. It was getting dark. There were no lights of any kind and you couldn't see your hand in front of your face. We had to carefully climb out of the car along a very shaky edge of the bridge and make our way around the car and then watch for other holes in the bridge as we made our way up the narrow road to the house. The car stayed on the bridge for the night. The next morning Jerry helped jack the car up so he could get a board under the front tire and make sure it stayed there to get the back wheels across.

Jerry and Carol were great hosts for a family of six. On a couple of occasions, we stayed in a little guest house and other times we occupied the upstairs bedrooms of the big house. When it got dark in the jungle, it was dark. Not a light anywhere. The darkness was so thick you could not see anything. Jerry would fire up the diesel generator and when everyone was safely tucked in bed, he would turn it off with a rope that hung in the upstairs bathroom.

The windows in the house were wire screens that took up most of the wall. It was heavenly when it would rain on the tin roof. You could not talk because the noise from the rain on tin was so loud. When it was not raining the night sounds of the jungle would sing you to sleep.

Carol had a steady flow of people from several villages who would come by her door. Sometimes they needed to have a wound dressed, or perhaps they had bananas or papaya or other fruit to sell and sometimes they just needed to talk. We were always amazed that no matter how busy Carol was she always was patient and took time to visit with them.

There were many adventures associated with our Dos Rios visits. We swam in the river, gathered stones from the river to polish, the kids jumped from the bridge into the river, except for Marshall. Matthew was hesitant as he stood on the edge of the bridge looking at the swift current of the river 30 feet below. Michaela decided he had hesitated long enough. She said a quick prayer and gave him a gentle push and he plunged into the river below. We walked to a nearby village and on the way, Michaela proceeded to step in a red ant hill. Instead of taking off on the run she stood in it while they bit her. Then there was the time a tarantula crawled out of some flowers on the dining table while the kids were playing a game. Michaela jumped up screaming and ran all the way upstairs.

On a beautiful hot day Jerry had hired two of the jungle Indians with their dugout canoes to take us down the Napo River. Marshall and I were in one canoe and Jerry and Jamie Kadle were in the other. It was easy going down because we were going with the flow of the river. It was a beautiful ride. Sometimes we would float along under a canopy of trees with beautiful butterflies and birds and other times we would hit the rapids and shoot between large boulders. When we reached our destination, a sandy beach where another river joined the Napo, we did some fishing, had a picnic lunch that Carol had packed, and swam. The current at the confluence of the two rivers made a huge whirlpool. Marshall got caught in the whirlpool and I thought he was going to drown. I could not get to him fast enough, so I prayed, and he was able to swim out of it. Our FAITHFUL God was watching over us. What had taken us about an hour going down river took us over three hours going back as our guides stood in the front of the canoe with a long pole and worked up a good sweat as they literally pulled us back up the river.

The other mission station in the Tena area was Pano, named for the Rio Pano that flowed just behind it. The station had been established by Bill and Mary Kadle. Bill built the house along with a church and school. Unfortunately, he died there early in his missionary career. His grave is across the road from the mission house along with a church and school. Bill was a strong believer in education and had established Christian schools all up and down the Rio Misahualli. The dirt road to Pano ended at the mission station. Prior to the road, and where the road is now, was an airstrip and the only way in and out of the area. Just beyond Pano was the village mission outpost of Shandia. This is where Betty Elliot started her missionary career and before she met Jim Elliot. We took the kids one day and along with Mary and her kids walked to Shandia from Pano. To get there we had to wade across a river up to Joyce's waist. We stopped along the way to visit Mama Rucca. This station sat empty after Betty Elliot left and Mary would walk in from time to time to visit with the people.

Mary stayed at Pano for several years after Bill's death. When the last of her children, Mary Beth, left for Quito for boarding school at the Alliance Academy, Mary decided it was time for her to leave as well. It was difficult for a single woman to maintain the house, church and school. Mary came to the Alliance Academy and worked in the library. Unfortunately, 15 years to the day that her husband Bill Kadle died Mary slipped to her death along the Shell Road after getting out of the car to stretch her legs as they were stopped at a landslide. This happened on a return trip to Pano for an anniversary celebration. What a sad day that was as it left the Kadle kids orphaned.

A Train Trip

There were other memorable trips almost too numerous to mention, but we cannot leave out the famous train ride from Quito to Guayaquil. This trip was on the Ferrocarril, a one-car train, with Ray, Eddie and Shelly Johnson from Butler who were visiting us. What should have taken us eight hours took 24. The route is a switchback railroad and winds its way along the valley of the volcanoes and through the Andes Mountains. We got stopped in one of the mountain towns because of a landslide caused by heavy rain. We sat up and slept on the train all night. It got cold once it got dark. There wasn't anything to eat except what the street vendors were hawking, and we were afraid to eat it not knowing if it would make us sick.

We got a little silly about two in the morning. Ray Johnson was standing on his head in his seat and Matthew had a dirty diaper that smelled up the whole train. One of the passengers, an older man, took his pajamas out of his bag and proceeded to put them on over his clothes. Then he sat all night saying his rosary. When we finally started on our way, at the area of the landslide the tracks were floating on their ties in the mud. It's a good thing we were only one car. On toward the plains and the coast we traveled through numerous banana plantations. We got into Guayaquil in time to be met by Carl and Ione Eckdahl, who took us to lunch, and by that time we had to go to the airport to catch our flight back to Quito. The Johnsons were leaving for the States the next day.

Colombia Trip

Some of our good friends and colleagues at the Academy were Dale and Wanetta Groeneweg. They were former missionaries to Colombia. We drove with them to the Colombian border and because of insurance had to leave the car in Ecuador. We took the bus from there to Cali, Colombia and then ventured to an Alliance mission outpost called Ambachico manned by Edwin, a single missionary from England. His work was among an indigenous tribe. They had horses at the mission station for everyone and we went up the mountain to a grassy meadow to ride. Marshall was not sure he wanted to ride a horse. We finally got him in the saddle and then he couldn't make the horse go. It was just plain stubborn. Mom to the rescue! She walked up to Marshall's horse and smacked it on the rump. It not only moved, it took off running with Marshall hanging on for dear life. It was all downhill and a scary ride for Marshall. He said, "I'll never get on another horse as long as I live." The only other eventful part of the trip was the bus ride back to Ecuador. The bus we were on stopped and made us get off and wait for the next bus. I guess we had too many people on the bus to go through a police checkpoint.

VI

The Real Reason we were in Ecuador

LEST YOU BE disillusioned, the reason we were in Ecuador wasn't tourism. We were there as leaders and teachers at the Alliance Academy. The Alliance Academy was founded in 1929 as a school for missionary kids whose families were involved in church planting across Latin America. It was a boarding school and by the time we arrived in 1975 the school had grown considerably and was also accepting diplomatic corps students and students from the international business community. Students had to have a passport from outside of Ecuador.

In my role as high school principal, I was the educational leader for 250 students and a faculty of approximately 30. All my teachers were on missionary allowances and we all earned the same cost of living salary. I was responsible for the academic program, discipline, scheduling, public relations with our sponsoring missions and serving as the assistant director of the K-12 school of over 550 students.

Joyce was the Alliance Academy's first Kindergarten teacher. The Elementary school was about 225 students K-6. Most grades had one section until 5th and 6th grades.

Setting Up the First Alliance Academy Kindergarten

Joyce loved the challenge of setting up the kindergarten. At first, she had to set up in a temporary facility. It was in an old high school portable building. Joyce started designing the furniture she wanted and the Ecuadorian workers in the shop at school built her the proper furniture for her classroom. The second year, kindergarten got transferred to another small portable across the soccer field on the elementary side.

In the small building next to the kindergarten there was a preschool for teacher's kids where Matthew attended along with several other little boys. They were full of mischief. The teacher would call them from the playground and then start counting. They had to be in their seats by the time she got to ten. They started scrambling and took off running. When the Alliance dorm was moved to the new facility, Joyce was given a large room in the old dorm building. This setting was like heaven after the small rooms she had started out in. She was able to develop centers, she had blowup figures to teach letters and lots of space for story time. She had two full-time helpers, Katie Miller and Marilyn Foster

Peace Corps Bible Study

While living in Jippi Joppa, Joyce and I hosted a Bible study in our home for Peace Corps volunteers. We would have them for several weeks before they went out to their location and any time they returned to the city. We made the contact through a Peace Corps volunteer by the name of John Hadley whom we met at English Fellowship Church. John had a passion for seeing his Peace Corps buddies find Jesus. None of them had any Biblical background. At the first meeting I asked them to share a "spiritual experience," thinking that would be nonthreatening. One of them shared that he was out in the forest when lightning struck a tree and he realized there was a powerful force of nature greater than man. This was an eye-opening experience for us and them. When it came time for Thanksgiving, they were all longing for home, so we served pumpkin pie. Just before they left for their allocation, we gave all of them a roll of white toilet paper to take with them. They had discovered the white toilet paper in our bathroom and were excited about it because all the toilet paper in Ecuador was purple and felt like sandpaper.

We lived in Jippi Joppa for two years before moving 10 blocks up Villalengua, from Avenida de Americas on the side of Pichincha an active volcano. We were just across the street from the Howards. We needed house help so we shared a helper with them by the name of Piedad. She cooked a great arroz con pollo and was sweet and loving with the kids.

On several occasions we drove to the top of Pichincha on a winding narrow road that clung to the side of the mountain. My first time to drive up was when my mom and dad came to visit. To say the least it was a white-knuckle ride. Dad clung on for dear life. At the top we could see all of Quito, the mountains beyond and watch the hang gliders.

Ecuadorian Christmas Party

One of the events that happened each year at Christmas on the elementary campus was what was known as the Ecuadorian Christmas party. One year, we had a group of students form a high mountain town called Tocahi off the back road to Otavalo. We learned that families were starving and only had the broad leaves of the aloe plant to boil and eat. Our family took the Christmas money that was sent to us by family and friends and bought large bags of flour, rice and sugar and broke them down into five-pound bags so each family would get one bag of each. Marge Sproxton and Ruthie Frederick helped us bake cookies. We made a bag of cookies and candy for each child that our kids handed out to them. We were told by the principal of the school who worked with us that not even the Catholic Church in the community had done anything to help families. This was one of many service opportunities that we tried to provide our family. We made regular visits to an old folks' home where our kids took flowers in homemade vases out of ketchup bottles to each person, played music, sang and read the Bible. The home was in need of repair and Michaela prayed every day that the people wouldn't get wet when it rained.

Christian Service Outreach

As part of the Alliance Academy faculty and staff, we were given the opportunity to be the leaders of a Christian Service Outreach group (CSO). This was truly a challenging and rewarding experience. We had a group of 10 juniors and seniors and could design our own types of outreach experiences. Our group was incredibly talented musically and in drama, so we purchased large puppets and they developed a puppet theater. We put on puppet shows in the Centro Commercial de Quito, a large shopping mall, at Christmas, along with the Academy Choir. We did puppet theater in several locations around Quito on weekends.

At the beginning of each school year, we planned a retreat for our CSO group for spiritual enrichment, teambuilding and planning for the year. One year we held the retreat at Papallacta, near a hydro plant that belonged to HCJB. We had the use of a large mission guest house and the thermal springs. We had taken the family with us as well and it was the trip where Skipper Pickle Eggs became famous. Skipper Pickle was one of our CSO members and Matthew liked the way he made eggs; thus, Matthew invented the name and it stuck.

Every year, each CSO group was allowed a weeklong trip. Our group did medical caravans with a team from Vozandes Hospital with Dr. Ron Gudarian and a couple of nurses. Our CSO kids served as helpers to the nurses and some of our students who were in advanced biology did all the microscope work to identify parasites from stool samples that the people would bring in on a banana leaf. We set up a clinic in an old wooden schoolhouse and saw patients all day long. They would stand patiently in line in the hot sun waiting to be seen by the doctor. I always served as the pharmacist and dispensed all the medicines from the prescriptions the doctor would write.

Sometimes we would have a dentist on the trip with us. One of our students, Chin Ku Kim, learned how to pull teeth by being an apprentice to the dentist. Most of the people who came with a tooth ache had very rotten teeth from chewing on sugar cane. We had little or no Novocain and often just held the patient down on a metal or a plastic chair while they had their tooth or teeth extracted. Chin Ku was like the pied piper and because he was Korean and funny the kids followed him everywhere. When he wasn't pulling teeth, he told flannel graph Bible stories under a tree.

On one of our extended trips, we flew our group into a jungle station called Arajuno from Shell Mera. We worked with a missionary couple who had several small children. We were flown in on Mission Aviation Fellowship (MAF) flights and conducted a week of VBS for kids, did soccer evangelism on a dusty street in the local community and held evangelistic meetings on the mission station at night. The five guys each took a night and preached, plus the whole group did several musical numbers. Joyce and I stayed with the girls in an unoccupied house left behind by the Shell Oil Company where we were met by an army of tarantulas and a large lizard. We could lie in bed and watch the tarantulas in the rafters. I guess the lizard was our friend. He knew where his next meal was coming from.

On the day we were to leave, thunderstorms began to roll into the area. The pilots of the small MAF Cessna planes were afraid they wouldn't be able to get us out before the storms broke so they called in back-up from Jungle Aviation and Radio Service (JAARS), the Wycliffe pilots and planes from Limoncocha. Even with that, I was left behind because there wasn't enough space. Genie Jordon, son of Gene Jordon, came back for me. On the way out, he flew me low over Palm Beach and the Curaray River where Jim Elliot had landed his plane and the five missionaries were martyred. We dodged thunderstorms all over the jungle on our way back to Shell.

I sat in the co-pilot's seat and watched the fuel gages keep dropping toward empty. So I ask, what happens if we run out of fuel? Genie said you see those big, tall trees with the flat tops down there? When I acknowledged that I did, he said I'll try and set her down as gently as possible in one of those. Fortunately, we made it. The tank in the right wing was completely empty and the left was barely showing above empty when we landed back in Shell.

Family Traditions and Fun Things in Quito

Some of the fun things we liked to do in Quito included going out to the Equator. On one of those trips shortly after we arrived in Ecuador, we had driven out on a Sunday afternoon. I had forgotten my wallet and driver's license and sure enough on the way home we got stopped at a police checkpoint. I tried to play dumb as though I didn't understand what the policeman was asking until our bright son Marshall from the back seat said "Dad, he wants to see your license." Then the police in perfect English asked me for it. I told him I didn't have it, but my wife had hers. He accepted her license and let us go with the admonishment to be sure I carried it when I was driving.

We had a tradition of strolling down Amazonas, the Fifth Avenue of Quito, at Christmas time. We liked to look in all the shops. Also, on Amazonas was the penthouse restaurant El Tartaro where we liked to eat on special occasions like birthdays and anniversaries. They had excellent steak and ceviche. There was always a fire in the fire pit as you stepped off the glass elevator. We enjoyed the Quito Days concert at the Sucre Theater on 6 December. Marshall didn't like the way Gene Jordon jumped around when he was playing the Marimba. The concert was organized for the city by HCJB in appreciation for granting them a license to operate the radio station that broadcast all over the world.

Special Friends

Eric Howard and Matthew were the same age and good friends. Vern and Bevan Howard were our good friends and when we got together, we loved to eat. Vern loved to grill meat. When we went to their house to eat, he would have two or three kinds. The Howards had Dachshunds and gave

Matthew one of their puppies as a gift. Here is Matthew with that black dog we called Scamp. He was a great friend and we all cried when he died

by being poisoned. We spent most of our holidays together and enjoyed great Thanksgivings over smuggled in frozen turkey. When we were together, we laughed a lot, usually at Vern's corny jokes.

We also spent great times in the home of Tommy and Millie Barry. Randy and Marshall were good friends. It seemed we always got together over a meal and Millie always made a batch of monkey bread. Millie and Tommy were always there for us and friends that we could unburden our hearts to about the struggles that we had at the Academy. We enjoyed camping trips to Cotopaxi sitting around a big bonfire trying to keep warm.

We had good times with Dave and Dorothy Yoder at the Wycliffe guest house. Michaela and Cynthia Yoder were good friends. We had the opportunity to meet many of the Wycliffe missionaries along with Rachael Saint. We also met Dayuma, the first convert from the Auca tribe, and her son Sammy.

Marj Sproxton and Ruthie Fredrick were great friends and the kids loved going to their apartment. They always had the kids stay overnight when we had late night events with Academy students, such as senior prom etc. They set up a bear hunt for the kids that they really enjoyed.

Ken and Marilyn Foster became good friends. Marilyn loved to cook, and we enjoyed many great meals at their home including Nigerian curry and cuscus. She and Ken had been missionaries in Nigeria where Marilyn had grown up as a missionary kid. Melissa and Valerie were good friends. Ken was coach of the cross-country track team and Marshall was part of the team. Ken was funny and sometimes plain juvenile. After Ecuador, we continued our friendship with the Fosters. Joyce and I visited them on several occasions while they were missionaries at Black Forest Academy in Kandern, Germany. We had a lot of excursions together in the Black Forest of Germany and Switzerland. One year they joined us for Christmas in Tuscaloosa and another year we did a beach trip to Gulf Shores. One of Ken's favorite phrases was, "where's the beach?"

Galapagos

One of the great privileges as a family was a Christmas trip in 1983 to the Galapagos with Tommy and Millie Barry and their son Randy. We flew from Quito to Guayaquil and from there to Porto Ayora where we boarded our ship. We arrived mid-afternoon on Christmas Eve. There were about 70 or 80 people on board. The kids were fascinated with the ship and explored every part of it. Matthew was the most intrigued and was all over the place. In his exploring he met the captain. Of course, by the end of the afternoon everyone knew Matthew. We were given an itinerary and learned that at the invitation of the captain there would be a midnight dinner to celebrate Christmas.

As a family we got all gussied up and arrived for the Christmas Eve dinner. We were welcomed at the door of the dining room by the ships steward, who informed us that Matthew had been invited to sit at the captain's table. He had been telling us this all afternoon, but no one believed him. When it became a reality our jaws dropped, and Joyce went into a tizzy. Then when she saw where he was seated, by the captain's lady friend, she was just sure he would spill something all over her lovely evening gown. She was so nervous she could hardly eat the lovely roast turkey with all the trimmings. Side note: Matthew made it without spilling!

After the dinner we left port and sailed through the night toward our first stop. After breakfast we were treated to beautiful views and a lot of small penguins. One of the highlights of the trip was the opportunity we had to board small boats at each stop and step foot on the various islands where we saw incredible wildlife. There were blue footed boobies, iguanas, sea lions, albatross and much more. The kids got to swim with sea lions in a lava hole on one of the islands.

On Santa Fe Island all of us except for Joyce and Mille got stuck with what seemed like a million sea lions. The small boats that they used to ferry us back and forth had broken down. The seals were relentless and kept barking at us. I think we were invading their space. By night fall we still hadn't seen a boat. We could see the lights from our ship, and then another ship came into view. Ours had sent out an S.O.S. Finally, in the dark of night along a shark-infested rocky coast a small boat arrived to rescue us. One of the sailors was guiding the boat in with a flashlight.

At one of the meals, I had gotten a bit dressed up in some new yellow pants. The meal that night was cow tongue in tomato sauce. I was sitting next to Tommy Barry and as he passed the platter to me all the tongue and tomato sauce slid off the platter into my lap. What a revolting development that was. My yellow pants were never the same.

Some of the highlights of the trip were the kids swimming with the sharks, climbing to the top of an extinct volcano, being chased by blue footed boobies, seeing the huge Galapagos turtles at the Charles Darwin Center and a host of other adventures. Meals were less than appealing. We had hoped for fresh seafood, and Matthew being his gregarious self, informed the cook that his mother was disappointed that there was no fresh fish. So, a couple of the sailors had fished off the back of the ship and the cook prepared a platter of fish and had it sent special delivery to the room.

On the seventh day we disembarked and boarded our flight directly to Quito on New Year's Eve in time to see the burning of the old man. This was a tradition in the passing of the old year to the New Year. The old man represented some part of life that people wanted to leave behind. Many of the old men were holding a liquor bottle. Some of these displays were very elaborate. The old men were made of stuffed clothes and very realistic. At midnight, the displays were dragged into the street and set on fire. Then those who had built the display would jump over the fire to cleanse themselves from the past. A cultural tradition.

University of Alabama Graduate Studies

During our time in Quito, we were provided an opportunity for further education taught by professors from The University of Alabama. They came to Ecuador three times a year and delivered graduate-level courses. Joyce started her master's degree and I did all my course work and took my comprehensive exams for my Doctorate. We hosted several of the professors in our home for meals. We have continued our friendship with Dr. Carrell Anderson. I had to return to the US to complete my degree. I needed to be on campus for two consecutive semesters, do my dissertation research and write my dissertation.

In the middle of all this learning, we had a short 6-month study furlough in 1982 in Alabama where Joyce finished her master's and I continued to work on my doctorate. Joyce had an internship to supervise student teachers, which she enjoyed. During those six months (January to June), we got snowed in with no electricity or heat and ended up staying overnight with the neighbor and his girlfriend. He put a fire in the fireplace and gave us the living room. We were renting a house in Northwood Lake in Northport, Alabama. Snowed in, in Alabama. What are the chances of that?

The kids went to public schools, which was a different experience and everyone made at least one good friend in the neighborhood. Michaela had a fight with the neighbor boy, Marshall got paddled at school, Matthew and his friends set the backyard on fire and I'm not sure where Melissa was hiding out. Matthew's bedroom was the laundry room off the kitchen. It was kind of like camping out.

Our last year in Ecuador and especially at school was difficult for us knowing that we were going to return to the US not to return to Ecuador. Each one of the four M's should write their own chapter about this time in our journey and the struggles they had in returning to the U.S. The reality of it all began to hit us when it came time to start selling furniture and preparing to pack.

The day we left Ecuador was an emotional day as we said goodbye to friends, to the Academy, and to Ecuador. I can remember weeping as we taxied down the runway for takeoff. My heart was broken with what I thought could have been a lifetime career as a C&MA missionary in Ecuador at the Academy. Bob Trempert had left Ecuador the year before we did. The school board had been given misinformation about me so I was not considered to become the director. The Board then chose Ben Schepens to be the new director at the recommendation of Bob Trempert. Ben was my high school science teacher and had no administrative experience.

I spent my last year as the high school principal, tutored Ben in what he needed to know to be the Director and tutored Dave Wilcox to take my place as the high school principal. This arrangement wasn't what I wanted, but it was what God wanted. Little did I know that God had prepared me for a greater worldwide ministry. I've often thought of the story of Joseph when he said to his brothers, "You intended to harm me, but God intended it for good to accomplish what is now being done..." Genesis 50:20 NIV Even though our hearts had been broken, we, like Abraham, were obedient and went to a place we didn't know. Hebrews 11:8 NIV. God had plans for us far beyond all we could ask or imagine. Ephesians 3:20 NIV. His FAITHFULNESS prevailed.

The Renicks Family Stateside

We had many things we wanted to do since the kids had never spent much time in the U.S. We landed in Miami and stayed with Jack and Sylvia Edwards. We always had such a great time at their home. Joyce and I went to Tony Roma's for ribs with Jack and Sylvia, but the kids chose McDonalds with Chip and Tim Edwards.

From there we flew to Orlando. The Edwards bought us a two-day pass to Disney World as a welcome home. We were met at the airport by Ron and Pris Wilson, college classmates. We stayed with them and they loaned us one of their cars. We spent two very full, long, and tiring days at the Magic Kingdom and Epcot. We flew from Orlando to Newark, New Jersey since my mom and dad, Steve, Diane, Tim and Paul were at Lake Hopatcong. This was one of those rare occasions when we were all together as a family. Steve and Diane were getting ready to return to Brazil. We all stayed in the lake house that Diane's parents owned. We had a great time together and said our goodbyes to Steve and family. We were not sure when our paths would cross again. We picked up the car that Steve and Diane had been driving on their furlough.

We went from there to Nyack, a short drive, where we stayed in Simpson Hall, my former dorm, and made excursions into New York City. Mom and dad accompanied Steve and Diane to the airport and then joined us at Nyack. We took the kids all over the campus to show them where we had lived, where we dated, where we worked and some of the fun places we liked to eat. We took them around Nyack, along the Hudson River to Hook Mountain. One night in middle of the night some students were cooking in the dorm kitchen and caught it on fire. The smoke alarms went off, the Nyack fire department came and we all raced out of the building. To this day, I have this mental image of my mom in her nightgown carrying her purse. Shortly after that, mom and dad left to go home and we started our excursions into New York City.

We showed the kids as much of New York City as we could get in in two days. The kids and I went to the top of the World Trade Center. This was before 9/11. We sat on a window seat with a glass floor and looked down the side of the building trying to find Joyce, who was too chicken to join us at the top. From there we took the Staten Island Ferry so they could see the Statue of Liberty. When Joyce and I were dating we would take the Ferry for a cheap date. Can you believe 5 cents a round trip? We also went out to the Statue of Liberty after we got the long view. We visited Ellis Island where my grandfather Renicks was processed as an immigrant when he came to

America from Scotland. The William Renicks name is now on the wall as a reminder of our heritage.

We did the typical touristy things. We walked down Wall Street, visited Rockefeller Center, The Empire State Building and went to the Summer Spectacular at Radio City Music Hall (the Rockettes were fantastic). We rode the subway and walked into Times Square. We had a fun time looking at the skyline of New York.

After New York, we went to Philadelphia where we stayed with Joyce's Uncle Dale and Aunt Alice Jones. May they rest in peace! We hit the highlights of Philadelphia. We went to Independence Hall and to see the Liberty Bell in Liberty Park.

From Philadelphia on our way to Washington D.C. we drove through the Gettysburg Battlefield where Abraham Lincoln gave his Gettysburg address.

> *Four score and seven years ago our fathers brought forth on this continent, a new nation, conceived in Liberty, and dedicated to the proposition that all men are created equal.*
>
> *Now we are engaged in a great civil war, testing whether that nation, or any nation so conceived and dedicated, can long endure. We are met on a great battle-field of that war. We have come to dedicate a portion of that field, as a final resting place for those who here gave their lives that that nation might live. It is altogether fitting and proper that we should do this...*
> *Abraham Lincoln*

You can't visit here without a deep sense of awe and reverence. We experienced the same feeling as we visited Arlington National Cemetery in Washington.

In Washington we stayed at a hotel, but often found it difficult to find our way there. Marshall was our navigator and was in the back of the station wagon reading the map. The only problem was that it was an old map and some of the streets had been changed or no longer existed. One night we ended up in a less than desirable part of town. We stopped at a gas station to ask directions. There were two or three young African American guys that came to the car to see what these strange white people were doing in their part of town. They took one look in the back seat at Melissa and Michaela and immediately replied, "Look at dem' sistas." I tried to get directions from them but couldn't understand what they were saying and frankly couldn't get out of there quick enough. We eventually found the hotel.

We were in Washington long enough to see all the monuments and visit the office of one of the Senators from Ohio who gave us a pass to the Senate. We stood in the gallery of the Senate and watched some of the proceedings. We visited the air and space museum at the Smithsonian for Marshall, went to Mount Vernon to visit the George Washington plantation home, watched the changing of the guard at Arlington National Cemetery, visited the grave of John F. Kennedy and walked around outside the White House. Ronald Reagan was President.

From Washington we drove to Rehoboth Beach in Delaware, where Joyce's family had rented a large house. This was the first time we had all been together since her dad died. We had a lot of fun playing games, swimming, strolling along the boardwalk, and taking turns cooking meals for the Armitage army.

Our Move to Alabama

From there we made our way back to Zanesville where we picked up a U-Haul trailer to take the stuff we had stored in Ohio to Northport, where we were going to be living. I was exhausted to start the trip but had to do all the driving because of the trailer. I remember stopping at a rest area and just flopping down on the grass and going to sleep. Some friends, Farrell and Judy Maxwell, whom we had met in Northwood Lake on our first six-month furlough, had moved to Texas and rented us their home. Marshall and Melissa left their mark on the house and car as they were learning to drive. This was the beginning of a whole new journey.

We knew that this arrangement was to be temporary. The C&MA had granted us a year study furlough with the stipulation that if we didn't stay with the mission, we would have to pay back all that they had invested into our education, which included our tuition, travel expenses and housing. This amounted to more than $30,000. Phil started his dissertation research at the University and was given an internship in the International Programs office. Joyce worked part-time at a day care center in Alberta City called Little Peoples to supplement our cost-of-living allowance from the C&MA. The kids started school – Marshall, Melissa and Michaela were at Tuscaloosa Academy, an elite private school, and Matthew went to Vestavia Elementary school.

Starting before we arrived home and continuing throughout the summer, we had been getting letters and phone calls from Gene Garrick, a board member of the Association of Christian Schools International (ACSI). I chose to ignore them because they were pursuing me to work for them. I was neither impressed with the organization nor did I want to work for them knowing that I would have to pay back the money for our education to the Alliance.

Through my previous connections with Dave Pollock, a dear friend, I was invited to be part of the first conference on missionary kids (ICMK) in Manilla, Philippines. The conference was slated to be held in November 1984. The Zanesville Alliance Church blessed me and paid for my entire trip.

Much to my surprise, when I arrived in Manilla, Gene Garrick, Bill Davidson, and Bill McKinley – all members of the ACSI Board of Directors – were at the conference. I had made a presentation in one of the plenary sessions and almost immediately following, the three of them descended on me like vultures. Gene wanted to know if I had been receiving his letters. Much to my chagrin, I had to tell him why I hadn't responded. When I told him I was not impressed with the services that ACSI had provided to the Alliance Academy, as a member school, he responded with, "that is exactly why we need you at ACSI." I did a brief interview with them and listened to them explain what the job would require. I felt it was a job I could do and likely enjoy.

I also had an interview with the head of a mission that was forming a school in China called the International Schools of China. There were a growing number of missionary families going to China who needed a school for their children. They were looking for someone to come and begin laying the foundation for this school. I agreed to reroute my flight home from Manila to Hong Kong to interview for the job, which was basically offered to me on the spot. I stayed with him and his family. He suggested that I call Joyce and see if she would be willing to move to China. When I explained the situation to her, I got an immediate and emphatic "NO." Her reasoning was that the kids were too close to graduation (Marshall was a senior and Melissa a junior) and because we had just uprooted them from Ecuador that it wouldn't be fair to uproot them again. They needed stability. I had to agree this was perfect reasoning and made a lot of sense. I was up for adventure and she was looking at it from a very pragmatic point of view. Typical of our decision making.

Paul Kienel President ACSI with Joyce and Phil

ACSI continued to pursue me and in January they flew Joyce and me to Hershey, Pennsylvania, to an ACSI administrator conference to meet Paul Kienel, Executive Director, for another interview. We also drove from Alabama to Gatlinburg, Tennessee to an ACSI administrator conference to meet Roy Lowrie, President of ACSI. At that point in time, ACSI had a two-headed leadership structure. The day we arrived home from Hershey, we learned from Melissa that Arnie Shareski, with the C&MA had called. He said he would call back the next morning to talk with us. Joyce took the call because I was at the University. Joyce accuses me of sneaking out because I didn't want to talk with him. She learned that he wanted to see if we would be willing to go to Bandung, Indonesia to a C&MA school there. We didn't feel led to Indonesia. It was only an elementary school and Melissa and Michaela would have to go to Dalat school in Penang, Malaysia, as boarders. We just couldn't do that to them.

After prayer and a lot of discussion, we decided to take the job with ACSI on the condition that they either pay for our education or work out something with the C&MA knowing that there was no way we could pay it back. We were confident this would be a major sticking point, so we put it before the Lord as our last-ditch fleece. Little did we know that Gene Garrick held credentials with the C&MA and was good friends with Arni Shareski. Much to our surprise and relief, the C&MA agreed to forgive one fifth of the debt each year for a period of 5 years if ACSI through me would provide priority service to all schools serving Alliance missionary kids (MKs). In 1985 we were placed on loan from the C&MA to ACSI, which continued for 22 years until we retired.

The New ACSI Missions Office

We bought a house in Northwood Lake that had a basement. We were on an inlet of the lake so the kids could get a boat in and out to the lake most times. The basement needed a lot of remodeling so we could use it as an office. ACSI advanced the money so we could make the modifications. We officially started with ACSI on July 1, 1985. We had no idea the journey that we were starting! On the first day of work for ACSI, Paul Kienel, Executive Director of ACSI and my boss, called us. We were having a huge thunderstorm and lightning hit a big oak tree in the back yard. The lightning came in on the phone land line and knocked the phone out of my hand. Paul would often joke about how powerful he was.

There were some conditions set out by ACSI: 1) we had to start out with the office in our home because of funding, 2) Joyce had to be my secretary because I couldn't bring another woman into our home, 3) the kids had to attend a Christian school, and 4) ACSI would provide us with a car.

Joyce at work in our basement ACSI Office

We checked out the main Christian school in town called West End. They were going through a lot of internal turmoil and it looked like they were about to close. So ACSI gave us permission to send the kids to a private school so they weren't in a public school. They were enrolled at Tuscaloosa Academy (TA). Because Marshall had taken all the classes in Quito he needed for graduation, except for a US government course, he enrolled in classes at the University of Alabama for credit. Marshall graduated in June 1985. Following his graduation, he left for Quito to be part of graduation with his class at the Alliance Academy.

During his senior year of high school at TA, he would wait in the gym and bring Melissa home from basketball practice. It was during these waiting times that he met Laurie Elizabeth McKenzie. The two became good friends and he took her to his senior prom. Her sister Cindy played basketball with Melissa. Marshall worked for Bama Bino Pizza that summer delivering pizza.

We had taken Marshall and the whole family to Covenant College in Chattanooga, Tennessee on Lookout Mountain. During that trip, after much negotiation with the President, Martin Essenberg, whom I had met at

ICMK in Manila, and the financial aid people we were able to make it work financially. They gave us some fantastic breaks because of our missionary status and Marshall's academic standing. Marshall took the CLEP tests in Spanish while at The University of Alabama, which gave him 30 credit hours, the equivalent of another major. We took Marshall to Covenant in late August where he met his roommate, Terry Pettit, and they roomed together all six years of college.

The Renicks Family Rejoined

Labor Day weekend 1985 we moved mom and dad from Ohio to a little house that they bought in Northport. They had been down for Marshall's graduation and were here for a week. Much to our surprise they bought a house. Joyce and I flew to Zanesville and loaded their stuff into a large U-Haul truck that I drove. Joyce drove their car and pulled dad's boat. We stopped just outside of Nashville and stayed overnight. We had put our clothes in the trunk of the car the next morning and walked across the parking lot to eat breakfast at Shoney's. Interestingly, mom had one of my old briefcases in which she had a stash of cash and all their important papers. It went with her everywhere like it was chained to her wrist, except when we went into Shoney's to eat. Mom accidently left the briefcase on the tongue of the boat. She didn't miss it until we had eaten and came back to the car. She was shocked to find it sitting there. I guess her hunger had temporarily seared her brain. Her FAITHFUL Lord came through for her once again!

Melissa started her senior year at Tuscaloosa Academy and discovered that it was difficult to establish friendships even with the girls on her volleyball team. I guess part of that was because it was difficult to break into established relationships. She also had world experiences from living in Ecuador that none of them could relate to. She still longed for her friends in Quito. In 1986 Melissa graduated from TA and I graduated from The University of Alabama with my Doctorate. Matthew said we were going to celebrate all day because I wouldn't have to study so much. Following graduation, Melissa went back to Ecuador and graduated with her class. We were so thankful to the Alliance Academy for accommodating kids who had left during their high school years and wanted to come back and be part of graduation with their friends.

During the TA awards ceremony of Michaela's sophomore year, she was awarded the Paul Bear Bryant scholarship much to everyone's surprise. She was the first girl and first non-athlete to ever be awarded the scholarship. Thank you, Mr. Garrison! This covered her tuition for her junior year.

The summer of 1986, Michaela and Melissa went to the C&MA Life Conference in Estes Park, Colorado, with the youth groups from all the Alliance churches in Birmingham. When Michaela got her pictures developed, there was a certain young man in every picture. We also learned that she had won a very prestigious award for a contest she entered. She was queen of the cow pie throwing contest. She was the only one who had prior experience. We made it a lot of family fun when we would take picnics to Cotopaxi. There were cow pies everywhere that had been baked hard by the equatorial sun, we learned to throw them like Frisbees. Thus, her experience paid off. Little did we know that the young man in the pictures would start dating Michaela and would one day become our son-in-law.

When Melissa came home from Estes Park, it was time to start packing her up for Capenwray Bible School in Carnforth, Lancashire England. She would be attending Capenwray founded by Major Ian Thomas. While she was getting ready to leave for England, Matthew had enrolled in TA, which was not a good fit for him. He did well but didn't really like the atmosphere. He spent his 7th and 8th grade years there. Matthew joined the swim team at the Northwood Lake pool. He was a good swimmer and was noticed by Nancie Blewitt, who asked him to join the swim team at The University of Alabama.

Melissa's International Travel

Melissa's first stop on her way to Capenwray was Germany, where she met her friends from Quito, the Fosters, who were teaching at Black Forest Academy in Kandan. Valerie and Melissa had been good friends in Quito and had dreamed of going to Capenwray together. Melissa and Valerie traveled by train to London where they were to stay with an older lady who was a friend of Capenwray. This was just an overnight to be ready to board a bus for Capenwray the next morning. She would live in a large room with six or seven other girls from various cultural backgrounds with whom she became good friends.

She went to Kandern, Germany to stay with the Fosters for Christmas. On the way, in a London train station, she left her bag hanging on the back of her chair while she went to a counter to order some breakfast. She returned to find her wallet was gone along with money we had wired her for her train ticket. The other kids in our family had given up some of their Christmas to make sure she had enough to travel. It so happened that one of the Canadian students traveling with them had a credit card and he was able to pay for her ticket. While in Germany the Fosters outfitted her with ski clothes and skis and she had her first experience at skiing in the Swiss Alps.

The name of one special friend, Ken Michell, appeared in a lot of her letters. We especially heard about long walks along the canal into the town of Carnforth. Then, just before she was to come home, after seven months in England, we received a letter telling us that she and Ken had decided to get married. She said they had been counseling with the principal of Capenwray, Billy Strachen, and he had advised them that they should marry. Well, that sent Joyce into panic mode. She would sit on Melissa's bed and cry and say, "Why am I getting this room ready, she's just going to leave again." I was a bit more optimistic in that I had pulled a similar trick on my parents by telling them that I had decided to leave Nyack and take the Queen Mary to England.

When we met her at the airport in Birmingham, I asked her if she had picked up her luggage and cleared customs with it in Atlanta. There was this blank look on her face and she said, "I wondered why it took people traveling with me so long to get to our flight to Birmingham. I just sat in the airport and prayed that if there was something I was supposed to do God, would you please take care of it." Classic Melissa! How many international trips had Melissa made and always checked luggage through customs? My reaction was that I was certain I would have to drive to Atlanta with her passport to claim her luggage. But we had to wait for the luggage to come off the belt before we could file a lost luggage report. Lo and behold Melissa's bags were the first to come off the belt. This was an answer to Melissa's *Hail Mary* prayer to a FAITHFUL God.

When she came off the plane, we never mentioned the letter with her marriage announcement. While walking to the baggage claim, she sheepishly said, "You know that my letter about Ken and I getting married was just a joke right"? We said, "Yeah, we knew".

International Conferences and PFO

In January 1987, Michaela, Joyce and I traveled to the Second ICMK Conference in Quito. Michaela went in lieu of her senior trip back to Ecuador because she didn't want to travel alone after graduation. She stayed with her friend Amy Mann while we were at the conference.

This was the anniversary month of the martyrdom of the five missionaries in the jungle of Ecuador by the Waorani tribe. At the conference we had a lot of indigenous music and testimonies by some of the members of the killing party. Our office had done all the registrations. This was also the first conference for boarding personnel and was one that I organized through our ACSI International office.

This year was also the first year for Pre-Field Orientation (PFO) at Taylor University. This was an orientation for teachers, boarding parents and their families to help in their transition to a new culture and to working with Third Culture Kids (TCK'S). The program was born out of my doctoral dissertation. Melissa went with me and ran the kids' program.

Valerie Foster lived with us that summer and she and Michaela worked at Kentucky Fried Chicken. Valerie was going to attend Messiah College in Pennsylvania. Melissa enrolled and started at The University of Alabama in her bachelors' program in Special Education. It was good to have Marshall home from Covenant College for the summer. He went back and worked at Bama Bino delivering pizzas.

Many Moving Parts

We found 1988 to be a busy year with a lot of moving parts. We moved the ACSI office out of our basement to a larger location and hired Joan

Gilchrist. We needed more help and extra space as the international work of ACSI was growing rapidly.

Michaela moved out of high school, graduating from Tuscaloosa Academy, and moved into Southeastern Bible College in the fall to be closer to Jeff Leonard, the young man in all the pictures from Life, the National C&MA youth conference. Her dorm room was an old Sunday school classroom from the church that owned the property before it became Southeastern Bible College.

Marshall moved to Georgia Tech to begin his studies in engineering. He and Terry Pettit found an apartment close to campus that had been an old schoolhouse newly remodeled. Matthew moved from TA to West End Christian School. This proved to be a good move for him socially, athletically and academically.

Mary Beth Kadle moved in with us for the summer. She had just graduated from the Alliance Academy and needed a home before moving on to Toccoa Falls College in Georgia. She stored all her belongings with us until further notice. She was an orphan. Her mom and dad had both died in Ecuador, her mother tragically on the Shell Road. Jamie and Terrilynn, siblings, came to get her for college and stayed the weekend. We had always stayed in their home in Pano.

Twenty-Five Years

We celebrated our 25th wedding anniversary on August 24, 1988. It was a ridiculously hot Alabama August day and our air conditioner quit. We couldn't get a repairman there quick enough to get it fixed before all our guests arrived. The kids had organized a small program. Marshall read a poem he had written, and Jon and Joan Gilchrist sang a couple of duets. My cousin Elaine and her husband Allen and my Aunt Jean came from Ohio. Our family, my mom and dad, Joyce's mom, her sister Beve and a small gathering of Tuscaloosa friends helped us celebrate. The kids made us a memory book with pictures and letters from friends far and wide.

ICMK Nairobi

Joan Gilchrist, Joyce and I were very busy in the ACSI office. I had been traveling both nationally and internationally speaking at ACSI conferences and conventions. Joyce and Joan were both working on laying all the groundwork for ICMK Nairobi that was to be held in November 1989. I had made my first trip to Nairobi in October 1988, along with Dave Pollock of Interaction International, to negotiate hotels and a location for the ICMK conference. We were expecting 700 participants. Dave had been a missionary in Kenya at Rift Valley Academy and knew all the people who would be the host school of the conference.

In September 1989, I received a disturbing phone call from Roy Entwistle, headmaster of Rift Valley Academy, our host in Nairobi, informing me that the convention center we had rented and paid a large deposit on was no longer available to use for the ICMK. President Daniel arap Moi of Kenya had basically taken over the convention center for a meeting of the Organization of African States. The hotels we had booked were all within walking distance to the convention center and several hundred reservations had already been made and paid for.

Paul Nelson of Wycliffe, one of our other partners, booked airline reservations for us and we immediately flew to Nairobi. When we were originally looking for a venue, we came up with nothing else big enough in the area around the hotels. Once on the ground, we began searching and still came up empty. The only venue in Nairobi big enough was the United Nations and they didn't let anyone use it unless related to the UN. Besides, it was several miles from the hotels in heavily congested traffic. As Paul and I were visiting Roslyn Academy, an International Christian School near the UN, I asked the kids in one classroom where they were from. One little girl said she was from Ecuador, so I asked her name and when she told me her last name was Valenzuela, I remembered that one of my former Spanish teachers at the Alliance Academy in Quito had taken a post at the UN in Nairobi. When I asked her if her father was Edgar she said yes and told me he worked at the United Nations. To cut a long story short, I was able to meet with Edgar, who introduced Paul and me to his boss, the Director of Operations.

Now the interesting thing was, Roy Entwistle, the Director of Rift Valley Academy was with us. He had expelled this man's son from Rift Valley, and I had fired Edgar Valenzuela from the Alliance Academy. The only way we had a chance at the UN was if God would intervene. There were a lot of silent prayers that went up in that meeting and God did intervene in a miraculous way. President Daniel arap Moi was embarrassed at the loss of the facility for our conference because he was to be the opening keynote speaker at ICMK and we were hosting him for a luncheon

Phil meeting with Kenyan
President, Daniel arap Moi

following the opening convocation. Not only did we get the UN, but they were not allowed to charge for the use of the facilities. The deposit we paid on the convention center was returned and used to pay for meals at the various restaurants in the UN complex for all 700 delegates. The Kenyan government paid for bus transportation from the hotels to the UN with a bus on standby for people who wanted to return to their hotel during the day. The venue was perfect for the kind of conference we had planned. We used the General Assembly Hall for all our sessions. This added yet another huge dimension to our faith journey. Praise God for his FAITHFULNESS to us.

On one of our free afternoons, we took a side trip to the Bomas of Kenya, which is the ultimate cultural experience in Kenya. The Bomas display the culture of several tribes of Kenya, including their typical village, dress and dance. They put on an incredible show of dance and drums. I thought I was sneaking down to the front row to get better pictures when all at once I was whisked onto the dance floor by a very scantily clad young woman. Flashes started going off all over the place because this tour had a lot of the conferees in attendance. Dave Wilcox always told me that the reason I hired him at ACSI was because he submitted my photo dancing with this young lady along with his application.

It was a very eventful trip. Joyce, Joan and I had to go early to get everything ready for the conference. On our flight to Nairobi, we had a stopover in London and since this was Joan's only opportunity to see London, we did a whirlwind tour that even included fish and chips by the Thames River. After the conference Joyce and I spent two days and a night at the world-famous Tree Tops. This was a very British place since Queen Elizabeth was here when she learned of her father's death and that she would become Queen of England. On our first afternoon, we had a welcome tea served on the rooftop observation deck.

We couldn't leave the hotel and were walked in under armed guard because of the animals. We were locked into the hotel and the animals roamed free. The facility was built on stilts looking out on a brightly lit watering hole. The animals came in at night for water. Our bed was next to the wall with a small window facing the waterhole so we could lie in bed and watch the animals. On the way to Tree Tops, we took a tea break at an old British colonial mansion.

On our way home, Joyce and I stopped in London for some R&R. We were tired. We stayed at a mission guest house and we just relaxed and made some side trips into London for sightseeing. We toured the Tower of London and got a peak at the Queen's jewels. We stood outside Buckingham Palace and watched the changing of the guard and people watched in Trafalgar Square and Piccadilly Circus. We also did a tour of Westminster Cathedral.

Our kids were all in their places and doing well. Matthew was highly involved in swimming. He swam every morning before school and every evening after school at the University Aquatic Center. We started a tradition of going to Gulf Shores or Orange Beach for family vacations. This tradition continued for many years even after the kids started getting married. Marshall even asked for Elizabeth's hand in marriage on one of those trips. Even after we moved to Colorado Springs, we would fly into Pensacola, Florida for our beach vacation.

Winds of Revolution and Changing World Order

At the end of 1989 there was a revolution taking place across Eastern Europe. The Berlin Wall had come down and dictatorships in Hungary, Romania, Poland and across Eastern Europe had fallen. We didn't realize the dramatic impact this would have on ACSI going into 1990. I didn't believe I would ever see this in my lifetime.

Standing on the verge of the new year we were about to experience many family events and milestones in ACSI. In mid-January I received a phone call from Gary Voss, the Headmaster of a member ACSI school in Delaware. He had a visitor from Romania in his office. The visitor, Petru Dugulescu, was a pastor from a Baptist church in Timisoara. He had been instrumental in leading the revolution in Romania. He led thousands of Romanians with a fiery speech and prayer in the central plaza in Timisoara. He believed strongly that Romania must initiate a Christian school movement if the youth were to be liberated from the grip of Communism and atheism. He extended an invitation to me to come and teach them how to organize a Christian school. Later, in early

April, Art Nazigan, an ACSI Board member and Henry Towes, Director of Black Forest Academy, joined me for my first trip to an area that had been behind the Iron Curtain for more than 40 years. This was a trip that would forever change me. It was on that trip that God gave me a scripture that put it all in perspective.

> *"Look at the nations and watch—and be utterly amazed. For I am going to do something in your days that you would not believe, even if you were told". Habakkuk 1:5 NIV*

In the early spring of '91 Joyce and I along with Henry and Margaret Towes took a trip to Timisoara, Romania, to meet with pastors and school leaders to plan for the first Christian teacher's conference for Romanian educators. At the border going from Hungry to Romania we were stopped for what seemed like hours over some new rule that had been instituted from the time we got our visas until we traveled. It seemed impossible to reason with the border guard. Margaret wanted to bribe them with cokes, but Henry wouldn't let her. After much prayer we heard the Hallelujah Chorus loud and clear. We were suddenly given our passports and told to go. We never did figure out where the music was coming from. It must have been a heavenly choir of angels. But to us it signified another one of God's timely miracles. His FAITHFULNESS was demonstrated once again.

Margaret Towes with Phil and Joyce at Romanian Border

We learned there were a lot of Christian teachers that had lived secret lives in the Communist system of education. Many of them didn't have a Bible. One woman we met had copied by hand the majority of the New Testament using a friend's Bible. She was overjoyed when we presented her with a personal New Testament and a set for her English class in a government school.

On our return trip back to Germany we took some detours. We visited Salzburg, Austria of Sound of Music fame. We took a carriage ride through the streets of Salzburg at night and stayed in a beautiful chalet on the side of the mountain. I remember the beautiful view, the fresh air, and the fact that the bed was short and the down comforter even shorter. If I covered my feet my shoulders were cold, if I covered my shoulders my feet froze. We also visited Innsbruck, Austria and the Neuschwanstein Castle in Germany on our way back. What an incredible engineering project that must have been. It was quite beautiful traveling through the Swiss Alps where the snow was still heavy on the mountains.

At the end of July, 1991, Joyce, Matthew and I, along with Gene Garrick and Jim Braley, left for the teacher's conference in Timisoara, Romania. This was a real milestone considering they had only been liberated from a Communist dictatorship for about 18 months. Our interpreter, Cornelia Stoika, had a son Matthew's age and he was able to spend time with him and take some side trips around the western part of Romania. Matthew survived on

Phil, Cornelia Stoika and Joyce
at Timisoara, Romania

bread, candy bars and Coke. This was a life-changing trip for Matthew with positive outcomes.

We invited two guests to the conference from the Ministry of Education in the Soviet Union and their translator through a contact we had with the Jesus film project. They seemed deeply engrossed in the conference. Following the conference Dr. Alexi Brudonov and his translator took me aside and asked for a private audience. In our private time he asked me if I would come to Moscow and teach his teachers how to teach like we were teaching the Romanian teachers. I explained that the reason we could teach the way we were in Romania was because the teachers held a belief in God. He acknowledged that his teachers were Atheists and Communists, then he followed that with *"just come and make them all Christians"*. He spoke of deep chasms that ran under all of Soviet Society and that their country was on the verge of collapse. This invitation led to the founding of the CoMission and the subsequent training of tens of thousands of Russian government schoolteachers in a curriculum of biblical morals and ethics.

Following the conference, Henry Toews and I left on a trip to Ukraine and Moldovia, all still part of the Soviet Union at the time. We were either brave or reckless, not sure which. We flew from Timisoara to Bucharest, that was an experience all its own. My seat only had one bolt holding it to the floor. This was the first and last rocking chair I ever had. After arriving in Bucharest, a man who had been at the conference met us and took us home for a scrumptious noon meal. Back to the airport, we flew on to Suceava where we were met by a Ukrainian couple who attended the conference. From there they drove us to Chernivtsi in southern Ukraine. To get there we had to cross a very difficult boarder. We were in a long line of cars and trucks that looked to be backed up for hours. Our driver got out and walked up the line to see what he could see. He found a trucker friend who decided to help move us to the front of the line. He had drivers move their vehicles by inches this way and that so we could get through. It was near two in the morning.

The guards were irritable and made us get out of the car. There was a guard on each side of the car with a German shepherd dog on a leash that constantly lunged at us growling and snarling. Another guard walked in the pit under the car checking for contraband or a person and this was after we had driven through and stopped in a water pit. Another guard interrogated the driver for more than an hour while we stood by the car and were subjected to lights that were brighter than day. We had a trunk full of contraband in that we had several boxes of Russian edition Children's Story Bibles. God was once again FAITHFUL in watching over us, the guards never asked to see what we had in the trunk. Can you imagine? God wanted those Bibles distributed in Ukraine. He was sovereign even over the Soviet guards. God's FAITHFULNESS prevailed.

While in Moldova we learned that all the borders form the Soviet Union into neighboring countries were closed. This was less than a month before the fall of the Soviet Union, so they were protecting their borders. The problem was that we were on restricted travel visas, meaning we could only be in the places our visa authorized and we could only stay for the time specified. Since we were stuck in Kishinev, Moldovia, with visas that were expiring, we tried to make the best use of our time by meeting with pastors and educators interested in starting Christian schools. We were basically planting seeds. I even did a baby dedication at one of the Baptist churches on a Sunday morning.

After several days and with expired visas, our local hosts found a diesel-powered car that was government issue with a Christian driver that spoke only Russian. Since both of us had to get back to Budapest, Hungary, they explained that they were sending us back up through Moldova and across southern Ukraine to a border town with Hungary called Chop. They were quite sure we could get back into Hungary from there. We traveled nearly 14 hours, first along the heavily fortified border between the Ukraine and Romania, and then through the night across the Carpathian Mountains on gravel roads avoiding as many villages as possible. It was raining and a thick fog settled across the mountains to the point you could only see about 10 feet in front of you. Each village had a military presence and we were stopped. The driver was the only one asked for papers. Praise the Lord for that. Not sure what would have happened had they asked for ours. I guess that is because it was a military issue vehicle and the fact that God was watching over us. We learned that our driver was a believer, so we sang hymns in English, German and Russian as we drove through the night, all blending beautifully. It also served to keep our driver awake.

The goal was to get us to the train station in Chop so we could get the next train to Budapest. The problem was that all the trains had been cancelled and there was wall to wall people sleeping on and under cardboard on the floor of the station. Using sign language, we convinced our driver to drive us to the border crossing. He was hesitant and said "nyet, nyet", no no and made the sound of an AK-47 with someone shooting us. He finely relented and we started down the road to the crossing. It was lined bumper to bumper with cars waiting to cross. Since it was early morning, people were out of their cars with their little charcoal burners making coffee and cooking breakfast. Since no one wanted into the Soviet Union, we traveled in the on-coming lane.

When we arrived at the crossing of course the gate was closed. My friend Henry, a very gregarious German, said, "I'm going to climb the gate, walk to the crossing point and see if they will let us cross." I tried to talk him out of it to no avail. I said, "Henry, they could shoot you." He said, "Then I guess I'll be out of the Soviet Union." Henry disliked the Soviets because of what they had done to his grandparents in Ukraine. I stayed in the car and prayed! He successfully scaled the gate and came back about 30 minutes later to say they were going to let us drive into the crossing area but that our driver had to go back. I don't know what we were thinking. Even if we did cross, there were no cars on the road and for sure we couldn't walk all the way to Budapest.

We were the only car admitted in. When we started unloading our luggage, another car from nowhere pulled in behind us. We were mystified because we hadn't seen anything but broken down East German and Russian excuses for cars. It was a black Ford Taurus station wagon with New Jersey license plates, and it was flying an American flag from the radio antennae. The driver spoke broken English. I asked if he was going to Budapest and when he said yes, I asked if Henry and I could ride with him? The answer was affirmative. Our Russian driver was ecstatic, pointing a finger toward heaven. We slipped him an extra $20 and piled into the angel-sent car and drove into the checkpoint. That meant we had to drive over a pit while a soldier checked under the car to make sure we didn't have someone or contraband hanging on underneath.

Remember, our visas had been expired for several days by this time. When our passports were handed to the guard, there were US, German, and Soviet passports. Immediately the guard said, "*Big problem, visas expired, must call Moscow*" and then he picked up the red phone and was talking to someone in Moscow. Our new driver took charge and smoothed everything over and we were on our way. We were welcomed with fanfare to Hungary. The driver drove down the road for several kilometers and suddenly pulled over and took the flag off his antennae. His remark was, "Those things sure come in handy when going through borders".

This Ukrainian/American driver drove us directly to the train station in central Budapest. We had time to get a day room across from the train station. We took showers, shaved and changed clothes. Henry got his train back to Germany and I caught a shuttle to the airport and made my flight back to the U.S. Have you ever heard of a chain-smoking angel? God provided us with one that made sure we got where we needed to be when we needed to be there. One more of those monumental FAITH building exercises in my life journey.

A New Era Begins

Another ACSI major milestone was the opening of the first ACSI office outside of the United States. I hired Stuart Salazar (28 years old), his wife Sheny and Patty Cifuentes. I had met Stuart on two occasions and was extremely impressed with his heart to serve the Lord and his humility. He had been a Bible teacher and head of the Bible Department at America Latina Christian School. He was let go and was searching for God's plan for his life. The office opened on April 1, 1990. Stuart was hired to be the Director for all Latin America. Stuart and Sheny have served faithfully advancing Christian schooling in Latin America, Cuba and the Caribbean for more than 30 years. What a blessing they have been to many.

Family Weddings and Events

Marshall and Laurie Elizabeth, just Elizabeth from here forward, had reconnected when Marshall was studying at Georgia Tech. They met in the mall in Tuscaloosa at Christmas and discovered that they both were living in Atlanta. Marshall took Elizabeth to Michaela's wedding and at the

reception she and Brent discovered that they knew each other from The University of Alabama. Back in Atlanta, Marshall and Elizabeth started seeing each other and going to church together, but Marshall declared they were just friends.

Jeff and Michaela were the first of our four to marry. I did all the flowers for the church, the reception and the bride and bridesmaids. I had a difficult time keeping the garage cold enough for the flowers because it was such a warm week. I had to wait to the last possible minute to load them in the car to take the flowers to the church in Birmingham. Matthew was helping me with the flowers, we were running late and I think the car sprouted wings as we made what is probably still record time for the trip from Tuscaloosa to Birmingham.

Joyce oversaw the cake top, which Michaela and her roommate had shopped for hours to find. She wanted the perfect top for the wedding cake. She had found a Precious Moments figure of a bride and groom. As Joyce was packing things to take to the reception the morning of the wedding, the bottom dropped out of the box and the Precious Moments bride and groom hit the floor and shattered into a million pieces. What to do? Michaela was totally unaware. Just the day before Joyce had seen one just like it in the Bible book shop in Tuscaloosa. She called immediately and had them put it aside for her. The day was saved and so was Joyce's neck. Joyce didn't share this with Michaela until several years later.

I guess we are prejudiced, but it was a beautiful wedding, with a beautiful bride. Everything came off without a hitch. No, wait a minute, there was a hitch. Jeff and Michaela got hitched.

Just a few days after the wedding, Joyce and I left for Hawaii for ACSI staff meetings. It was our second trip to Hawaii. Joyce and I stayed after the meeting for a few days after the stress of marrying off our youngest daughter and just to try and catch our breath. The first six months of the year had already been a whirlwind. We rented a car and drove all the way around the island of Maui, even on roads that were marked no entry. When did I ever let that stop me? We enjoyed visiting a cultural center that celebrated the culture of the Islands of the South Pacific. We didn't any more than get home and I left for PFO. Joyce started helping Melissa find a wedding dress in planning for a December wedding. Joyce remarked, "I don't think I can do this again," but you do what you must do. Wedding plans were getting underway.

Melissa had met a young man through her friends at Campus Crusade and they had become friends. Sometime later we were invited to a 5th Quarter party following an Alabama football game. We found it interesting that said young man, Brent Jean, spent most of the party talking with Joyce and me. He wanted to know all about our time in Ecuador. He hadn't asked her out yet, so I guess he thought it was a good idea to get to know her parents and a little of the family history. Her first date with Brent was to his office Christmas party at Ernst and Young. Melissa was just sure she didn't have anything good enough to wear. She borrowed a sleek black dress. She was a knockout. Her Uncle Dale and Aunt Connie were visiting the night Brent came to pick up Melissa. Her Aunt Connie said she wouldn't have her feelings hurt if Melissa didn't stay to visit if she married the guy.

Marshall had a medical emergency and called his mom to say that his left arm was swelled up the size of a football. It was inflamed with infection. He had been to the student medical center on campus. They gave him some Benadryl and it had no effect, so Joyce said, "get yourself to an emergency room." Elizabeth and his roommate went with him. He had been bitten by a brown recluse spider. He was allergic to penicillin and that was the preferred treatment. The doctor called Joyce to discuss the protocol. Joyce decided to go ahead with the treatment. Elizabeth stayed with him through the night to make sure he didn't have a reaction. Of course, I was traveling internationally and found out about all the drama when I got home.

Joyce and I went to Guatemala for the first ACSI teacher's conference in the fall of 1990. Stuart and Sheny were very new to this whole process so we pitched in and helped them get everything set up and ready. They had done a great job of organizing. Bud Schindler from Dayton Christian Schools was there as one of the keynote speakers. Following the conference, we took a side trip to Lake Atitlan with Stuart and Sheny and their two

little kids. This was just the first of many trips to this beautiful destination. One of our all-time favorites in the world.

Just after Christmas, December 29, 1990, and six months after Michaela's wedding, Brent and Melissa were married! I think Brent planned this so he could get a full year of tax exemption for two days of support. They were married at Circlewood Baptist Church and left for the Birmingham airport in Brent's convertible with Melissa's new bra flying from the antennae. With friends like that, who needs enemies. They were off for a ski trip in Colorado for their honeymoon. I did all of Melissa's flowers as well. It was much easier keeping them cold in the garage in December. They settled in an apartment in Bessemer. Melissa still had schooling to complete at The University of Alabama.

In May, Marshall graduated from Covenant with a BA in Christian Liberal Arts. It was a beautiful ceremony with a bag piper leading the graduates into the hall. In June he graduated from Georgia Tech with a BA in Engineering. We had seats in an upper deck of the arena for the ceremony and it was HOT! Following the ceremony, we went back to his apartment and began cleaning out and packing up his stuff to return to Tuscaloosa. We got rid of an old dirty white round chair by the dumpster. Brent came carrying it back saying look what I found. We told him we didn't want it and if he did, he had to take it back to Birmingham. My mom and dad were with us, so they took Matthew and headed back to Tuscaloosa. When we arrived home, mom, dad and Matthew weren't there. Now remember, folks, this was the age before cell phones, so we didn't know their car broke down and they were stranded along the way.

Marshall and Elizabeth were engaged while on a family beach vacation in 1990. Marshall wanted to take her on a stroll along the beach at sunset, but Elizabeth didn't want to go because she didn't think they should leave the family. We all knew why he wanted to take her for a stroll so we had to convince her that it would be fine for them to go. However, it didn't happen until the next morning.

On June 29, 1991, Marshall and Elizabeth tied the knot at Calvary Baptist Church, Elizabeth's home church. I did the flowers for their wedding as well. Trying to make bouquets big enough to show up in that large church was a real challenge. They left the morning following the wedding for an Ecuador honeymoon. Marshall was excited to show her where he grew up. I left almost immediately for PFO for two full weeks.

Africa on the Horizon

Jeff and Michaela were off to Cote de Ivoire (Ivory Coast) on a survey trip. Jeff had felt called to Ivory Coast, West Africa. He was hoping to teach in the C&MA Seminary. They had contacted one of the C&MA missionaries who were to meet them at the bus station. There was no one there when they arrived so Jeff stayed with the luggage and tutored Michaela in French, as what to say to a store clerk when asking to use the phone. She practiced it all the way to the store and tried her newfound language out on the clerk. He appeared not to understand a word she said, so she got really frustrated and started speaking Spanish. Finally, the clerk said in perfect English, "What language are you speaking lady?" (As related by Michaela).

Milestones and Moving Pieces

Joyce left the ACSI office and went back to teaching kindergarten at American Christian Academy. She felt she had put in her time and after all teaching kindergartners was her first love. To take her place, Elizabeth came to work at ACSI to be the office receptionist and direct all the activities of the CoMission.

Michaela graduated from Southeastern Bible College in May 1992, in their beautiful chapel with Dr. Talley presiding. Jeff had graduated a year earlier and was serving as the youth pastor at Westside Alliance Church. Following graduation, they packed up and moved to Nyack where Jeff started his M.Div. at the Alliance Theological Seminary (ATS).

Matthew graduated the same year from ACA. He had become a legend as the only basketball player ever to dunk the ball. Dan Carden, Headmaster, spoke a verse of scripture over each graduate. For Matthew, he used Proverbs 13:1: "a wise son heeds his father's instruction." Dr. Carden spoke of Matthew as being a wise young man who made his father proud. Matthew had looked at several colleges and decided on Southeastern

Bible College because it was small and had a major in secondary physical education. The only problem was they didn't have enough students for the program, so they cancelled it. That was a huge disappointment for Matthew.

I was off on an international trip to Moscow and Joyce had taken him to Southeastern to register. It was only the second day of the semester when I arrived home. I was exhausted and when Joyce picked me up from the airport, we decided to stop by the college so I could see his room and see how he was doing. We planned to take him to get something to eat. On the way to the restaurant Matthew sat in the back seat and cried. So instead of going to eat we went to an area on 280 near what is now the Summit to a nice business park with fountains. He sat and poured out his heart and informed us he wanted to quit. I discouraged that because we had always told the kids that if they started something, they had to finish it. In the middle of our intense discussion the sprinklers came on and gave us a little comic relief, much needed. We got soaked.

We got something to eat and took him back to Southeastern and I told him I would come up the next day and we would talk with Dr. Bette Tally and see what we could work out. He agreed reluctantly to stay the year because he would have to take basic freshman courses regardless of where he went. The following year he transferred to the University of Montevallo. After two or three tries at University, Matthew decided that it wasn't for him, so he quit and went to work.

With all that had been happening in ACSI, I felt like I needed a vacation. This had been one of the busiest years yet for international travel with new initiatives in Eastern Europe and the former Soviet Union. Then out of the blue we got a call from Ken and Marilyn Foster asking us to come to Nice, France. O-la-la, the French Riviera! Did we hesitate? NO! The same evening, I had obtained award tickets on Delta direct from Atlanta to Nice. Ken and Marilyn had secured the home of an IBM executive through a graduate of Black Forest Academy who was staying there. It was a large chateau. Our bedroom had large arched floor-to-ceiling shutters that opened onto a balcony looking out over the Mediterranean. We had a private pool in the backyard and we were close to the beach, which we didn't realize was topless until I was taking a shower on the beach provided for beach goers. When I turned off the water that had been pouring over my head and looked up, I got a very rude semi-nude awakening. The woman showering across from me had appeared from somewhere and provided me with a shock while Joyce, Ken and Marilyn watched my reaction. Could it be because I was so well outfitted by Matthew? Or was it my amazing physique? Matthew wasn't about to let us go to such a chic place with our old shorts and tops. He was working at Cycle Path and got us some good discounts. Interestingly, my shorts matched the ones that Ken was wearing.

The chateau owners had a speed boat that we decided to take out on the Mediterranean. As we were trolling along, we were approached by the French Coast Guard who informed us we needed to get it off the water because the license had expired. It was a good thing that the Black Forest grad spoke fluent French. We didn't waste any time.

We took a couple of side trips to Monaco and spent time looking at some mighty expensive yachts with the owner being served dinner on the upper deck by servants with white gloves. This is after all a destination of the rich and famous, of which we were neither. Joyce and Marilyn paid a visit to the Palace. Princess Grace and Prince Rainier reigned over Monaco. Ken and I made a visit to the local stadium to get tickets for the premier track and field event following the Barcelona Olympics. We were excited to get to see Carl Lewis run. It was truly a special event with the gold medal athletes from the Olympics. Ken bought at least 4 tee shirts after Marilyn had told him not to because he already had plenty and didn't need more. On the drive back to Nice, Ken kept pulling them out from under his seat as he was driving a very winding mountain road. He kept saying, "Well look what I found." It was a riotous drive home as we all laughed until we cried.

We're Grandparents

We began 1993 with a bang, an incredibly happy bang. Our first grandchild was born. *Woo Whoo* we're grandparents! Michael Brent came into our world on the evening of February 23rd. This was a BIG event, a BIG deal! We made it to the hospital that night and were able to see him shortly after he was born. When I went home, Joyce stayed with then for a few days to help Melissa take care of Michael. Joyce spent a lot of hours playing Scrabble with Brent. She found out what a good player Brent was. Brent had learned to play by playing against himself at all four positions.

We were surprised in early March with what might be called a once in a decade snowstorm. Melissa and Brent had come to Northwood Lake with Michael, Michaela flew in from Nyack to see Michael. Marshall and Elizabeth had come over and it started snowing. The mayors of Northport and Tuscaloosa panicked and closed all the roads and bridges, so everyone was trapped at our house. Brent took Michael out on the deck so he could experience his first snow.

New Discoveries – New Destinations

1993 was a busy year for me, I had a lot of travel on my schedule as ACSI was expanding rapidly around the globe. In addition, the office had grown as Richard Edlin, from New Zealand, came on board as my assistant. We, along with the Jesus Film Project and Walk Thru the Bible, partnered in the formation of the CoMission to train Russian government schoolteachers to teach a curriculum of morals and ethics based on the Bible. Teams of Christian teachers from the United States traveled to various cities across Russia to meet and train Russian teachers in a convocation. Joyce and I were part of a trip to the former Soviet youth camp called Orlyonok on the Black Sea. I traveled to Pushkin, Moscow, St Petersburg and Murmansk for other convocations being held across Russia. Marshall and Elizabeth also travelled to Eastern Russia with the CoMission to Vladivostok, Magadan, Irkutsk and Lake Baikal.

One trip that stands out to me was my trip to Irian Jaya. This was on my bucket list of places to visit because of the significance of this part of the world in our family's history. Joyce's Uncle Frank and Aunt Wilma Ross had served as missionaries there for many years with the C&MA. There had been great emphasis placed on this part of the world as missionaries began reaching lost tribes of primitive stone-age peoples. Some were headhunters!

I flew into Jayapura where I was met by Alex Valley, head of the Sentani Alliance School. From the airport we made our way to Sentani where I had the privilege of visiting two MK schools. I stayed at the C&MA guest house with John and Mary Hazelet who hosted me. I was not accustomed to taking malaria medication and Mary was so concerned that she made me tea by boiling the young leaves of the Papaya tree. It was awful, but she assured me that it was as good as any malaria medicine. It sure tasted like medicine. I flew with MAF into the interior to Wamena. I visited several mission schools for the nationals in the Wamena area and then flew to the C&MA station at Pyramid.

I flew up the Iloga valley over the top of many Dani villages with their sweet potato fields and pens of pigs. These were the two staples of the nationals. To land at Pyramid, since the airstrip was on a 45-degree uphill slope, the pilot had to open his door and stick his head out so he could see the ground to land. All I could see sitting in the co-pilot's seat was the sky. I had a great visit with Bill and Mary Sunda. Mary had baked an apple pie for my visit. The best food I'd tasted on the whole trip. I spent some time advising them on the Christian school they had started. My return trip to Jayapura was on a government plane hauling barrels of gasoline in the front of the plane, eggs and newly hatched chicks in the middle and I had a seat in the far rear of the plane. We bumped along over the mountains and I wondered if I'd die with fried eggs and feathers.

In September I took what was the first trip for a student international representative to Moscow. We had a contest among students in ACSI schools to see who could multiply a dollar and use it to make the most impact. Janelle Adderly won the contest and a trip to Moscow. She along with her mother Susan accompanied me on what for Janelle was the trip of a lifetime. She used her talent of interpretative dance in each of the newly formed Christian schools that we visited. We also visited several historic sites in Moscow, including the Kremlin and the cemetery where all the famous people in the history of Russia are buried, including Nikita Khrushchev, former Premiere of Russia. I can remember that during my senior year of high school in 1960, Nikita Khrushchev stood before the United Nations in New York and pounded his shoe on the lectern and shouted, "We will bury you." At the cemetery, I took off my shoe and pounded it on his gravestone and said, "Sorry, we buried you." Ray and

Cindy LeClair, ACSI Directors for Russia, were our host and hostess and took us all over Moscow.

For Christmas we received a surprise gift in the form of a fury, wiggly little black puppy that we named Max. He was a faithful companion for 14 years. May he rest in peace. He is buried in the backyard of our house at 1097 Golden Hills Road in Colorado Springs with his toy and wrapped in his blanket.

Close Friends and Family Happenings

As we started 1994 it began on a sad note. Our dear friend and colleague Margaret Toews, who had worked tirelessly in helping he husband Henry start the ACSI office in Budapest, passed away in Winnipeg, Manitoba, Canada. Joyce and I flew to Winnipeg for her memorial service. It was a bitterly cold April day. I can remember walking behind her casket as the snow crunched under our feet from the church two or three blocks to the cemetery. We had sweet fellowship with the family before returning home.

At the end of the school year, Joyce quit teaching Kindergarten and came back to the ACSI office in preparation of our move to Colorado Springs and to help manage expanding programs in the office.

It had been almost 10 years since mom and dad moved to Northport. They were a great help in looking after the kids when Joyce and I traveled together. Matthew loved his grandpa and the two were good fishing buddies. Matthew has kept some of his grandpa's fishing gear. It was so good to have them close, especially for the Sunday dinners that mom cooked and they were great dog sitters for Max. He loved going to their house but was ready to go home by 5pm. He would be sitting by the door waiting for us. Dad and mom were convinced he could tell time. God was so good to give us mom and dad for these years since we had been separated for so many years while living in Ecuador. With Steve and Diane and their boys in Brazil, mom and dad had sacrificed a great deal by only seeing their grandchildren occasionally separated by years.

Jeff and Michaela made their first trip to Israel with Dr. Bryan Widben, one of Jeff's professors at ATS. Dr. Widben instilled in Jeff a love for the Jewish people and Israel. This was just the beginning of many more trips that Jeff would lead. Dr. Widben was also instrumental in helping Jeff get into Brandeis University on a full ride scholarship. He was the only gentile in a Jewish Old Testament program.

On September 14, 1994, Melissa and Brent gifted our family with Brandon, our second grandson. This was a busy time! Melissa was at the hospital, Joyce was at the house with Michael, I had my mom and dad to take to an eye appointment in Birmingham and Susan Adderly (Mathis) to the airport. What a whirlwind. By the time I got back to Brent and Melissa's house with mom and dad, Brent was calling to say come to the hospital. The baby we had been waiting for had finally decided to arrive. This made our Christmas extra joyous.

There were exciting changes taking place at ACSI and in my life. The Mission's Office became the International Ministries Office, can you imagine that in Northport, Alabama? My title changed from Mission's Director to Vice President of International Ministries and I got a pay raise.

Matthew was home from Montevallo and getting ready to enroll at Shelton State Community College. I guess you could say he was a typical missionary kid having gone to three different colleges in three years. He did have a varied experience.

New Old Beginnings

1995 was a big year for me as the VP of International in the ever-expanding world of International Ministries. I hired four new people all to begin their work in Colorado Springs. Everyone in the Northport office resigned and Joyce and I went back to our humble beginnings in the basement of our house. ACSI had granted us the opportunity to stay in Northport due to mom and dad's health until we could figure out how to care for them. They weren't up to a move to Colorado because of dad's health. In December dad had open heart surgery and spent Christmas in the hospital. By this time, I was traveling to Colorado Springs one week out of every month, which took up a lot of my travel time so overseas trips were limited.

In November 1995 ACSI held the first teacher's conference in Ukraine. The conference was exhilarating. The opening session was conducted in the dark with a few candles on the platform. The teachers were like sponges, soaking up everything they possibly could and taking notes on everything. All of them had graduated from universities where the prevailing philosophy was Marxism and Leninism. To hear the truth of God's word and have it applied to teaching was a new revelation to them. At the close of the conference, all 11 presenters had tired of the steady diet of Borscht and bread, so we decided to load into the ACSI van, which was more than well used and abused. We had decided to go into Kiev for some pizza. As we were leaving, the weather had turned nasty with rain and then freezing rain and cold.

Just before a Ukrainian police checkpoint going into the city of Kiev, the van hit a patch of black ice and began skidding. Vanya, our driver, tried his best to get the van under control but to no avail. The van skidded down and embankment and flipped onto its side. There were no seat belts, so we were all thrown around the inside of the van. Priscilla Pop from Romania and Ed Balzer from the ACSI office in Hungary sustained neck injuries and had to be taken to the hospital. We pealed out of the van one at a time crawling through an open window on the driver's side, the upside of the van. Once we were out of the van, police officials had arrived and made us stand in the snow and freezing rain while they argued who was at fault. They tried to say that Vanya was drunk. Ray LeClair, the ACSI director for Ukraine and Russia, sat in the warmth of a patrol car for what seemed like hours arguing with the official. Some of the other officers built a fire and stood around it smoking while we were freezing. Because we were all foreigners, our accident was brought to the attention of the Minister of Foreign Affairs. In fact, they got him out of bed.

We never did get pizza and were taken back to our rooms at the conference center with nothing to eat. We had a phone in our room that didn't work the whole time during the conference, but when we returned from the accident, I picked it up just to see, there was a dial tone and we were able to get through to ACSI and Melissa. Then it went dead. Everyone was fine and miraculously we all got home in one piece. *"The LORD will keep you from all harm—he will watch over your life; the LORD will watch over your coming and going both now and forevermore".* Psalm 12:7-8 NIV

In December we went to Winter Park, Colorado with Brent and Melissa so they could ski. We took care of the boys while they skied. We decided to get the boys into their snow suits and car seats and take them to the small town of Grand Lake. We rented a sled so we could pull them around the streets that were packed with snow. Michael would have nothing to do with the sled. As quick as we would put him on it, he was off. He decided he liked walking behind the sled better. Brandon loved the sled and the faster I pulled the louder he squealed. That was when I still had enough lung capacity to run in the high altitude. It's interesting that Winter Park is on State Route 40. If you followed it far enough East, you would come to the farm where I grew up.

Jeff graduated from Alliance Theological Seminary (ATS) in May and he and Michaela moved to Boston. They moved into a first-floor apartment in Belmont. Jeff started Brandeis that fall and they started attending an Alliance church in Melrose. Michela took a job working for Dr. Rosenthal doing his medical records. He was an interesting character and she put up with a lot.

A Patriarch Meets Jesus

1996 was a year of deep sadness. The patriarch of the Renicks family went to be with Jesus on February 12. After his open-heart surgery, the doctor had told us that if dad didn't make it, it wouldn't be because of his heart. The question was would his lungs handle the new rich flow of blood. As it turned out, his lungs couldn't handle it and he died of congestive heart failure. I'm convinced it was because of all the years he had been a heavy smoker, even though he had quit when he became a believer 40 years prior. One of my fondest memories of this time was when the whole family gathered around his bedside at the hospital. He looked at each one of us, calling us by name and said, "I'm going to heaven, will I see you there?" I had ACSI staff meetings at Assilomar, California and was reluctant to go, but dad encouraged me to go. When I told dad goodbye at the hospital before I left, I had the feeling I wouldn't see him again this side of eternity. I was notified the first evening of staff meetings that he was critical and not expected to make it much longer. I was able to catch a redeye special out of San Francisco and unfortunately dad passed while I was in the air. I've always said we passed each other in the air.

Dad never was a very affectionate father. It wasn't until I was an adult and we went to Ecuador in 1975 that I ever had him tell me that he loved me. He was zealous for his faith and worked tirelessly at the Zanesville C&MA church. He was faithful to the commitment he and mom made at Beulah Beach Bible and Missions Conference so many years before. We always knew that he and mom prayed for us faithfully. He always reminded the Lord where we were when he prayed. We would miss dad's prayers.

Following dad's death, we knew that we would have to make the move to Colorado Springs. We busied ourselves getting the house ready to put on the market and up for sale. With the move, that would leave Matthew homeless. We were selling a house and looking for a small house to buy so he would have a place to call home. We were able to get a loan on our signatures to purchase a small house on Circlewood Dr. in Tuscaloosa. We did a lot of cleaning and painting to get it ready for him to move in. Matthew Tierce became his housemate and rented the second bedroom.

More Grandchildren and a Move

At the end of August, while we were in a great state of flux life just kept rolling on. Moses and Apple Umoh were visiting us from Nigeria so we could produce a mission's video with them. David Webb was the producer. During this time Michelle Brianna was born on September 10, 1996. We were so excited we finally got a girl. Moses and Apple went with us to the hospital in Birmingham to see her. They were thrilled and every time we talk with them, they always ask about Michelle. Moses said a wonderful prayer of dedication over Michelle. Michelle, you were blessed by the Rev. Dr. Bishop Moses Umoh of Nigeria.

A few weeks after Michelle was born Brent and Melissa packed up and moved to Franklin, Tennessee. They lived in a small apartment while the house they were building was finished. Joyce fretted over them living in this second story apartment with steel steps. How would Melissa manage getting all three of them up and down all those steps? She did!

I was in Colorado Springs on a beautiful fall day. I had been looking around for a house to purchase. Dave Wilcox told me of an Alliance couple from C&MA headquarters who were leaving to be missionaries in Russia. I went to look at the house and fell in love with it. They hadn't put the house on the market and agreed to hold it until Joyce could get out to Colorado Springs the next month for her to see it. It was a five-bedroom four bath house on a beautiful corner lot.

The house had been the model home for the development. It had high ceilings, a stone fireplace, a large downstairs bonus room and a large kitchen with a small sitting room with another fireplace. It was cozy. It had a large space under the steps in the downstairs family room that the grandkids loved to play in. It was the first place they would go when they came to visit. There was a small hat for a Mr. Potato head and Brandon would balance on his head and walk all over the house.

The setting for the house was in a canyon with beautiful rock formations and a park a half a block away. It had trees. It was perfect. The house was just what we were looking for, but we hadn't sold our house in Alabama, so Doug and Joan Wicks agreed to rent to us until we sold ours. Grandma Armitage came to visit and to help us celebrate our last Christmas in Alabama.

Early in January '97 the three M's - Margaret, Martha, and our faithful dog Max - accompanied us to Colorado. We crowded into the Isuzu Rodeo after the moving van had been loaded with all our earthly belongings, including our blue Honda. We knew we had a long trip ahead of us and uncertain winter weather. We stopped for a couple of days in Franklin to celebrate Melissa's birthday.

When we got back on the road, we headed for St. Louis to get on I-70 west to Denver. By the time we got to Kansas City, we were battling trucks galore and icy roads. We had to spend the night because the interstate was closed due to ice and high winds. When we did get started the next day there were 18-wheelers on their side in the median and off the side of the road. We drove straight through to Colorado Springs. It took us about 14 hours due to bad road conditions. We didn't get into Colorado Springs until about 11pm, where we found a motel close to the house. The movers arrived at the house to unload on Monday, Martin Luther King's birthday.

Besides our house furnishings, we also had the office furnishings and files that needed to go to the ACSI office. When we got to the office to unload, it was closed in observance of MLK's birthday. We were finally able to get hold of Dennis from the warehouse to come and open for us. We were sure glad to get to Colorado Springs and get in our home. I started work at ACSI HQ and came to appreciate having a close colleague, namely Dave Wilcox, to bounce ideas off. However, there were too many people looking over my shoulder and scrutinizing my work. I was used to making my own decisions and moving forward with plans. Now I had to get permission. My general philosophy had always been, it's easier to ask for forgiveness than permission. I guess it still is!

Our moms were a great help in getting us unpacked. They left to go home the next week. Our first visitors were Brent and Melissa and the kids for their annual ski trip. We had great fun with the kids while they were off skiing and celebrated Michael's fourth birthday. We were at the dinner table and for some reason not known to us, Michael was frustrated. He stood on his chair and emphatically stated, "I've had it with the French, the men and the women." We had no idea where that came from until the next day when Joyce was watching *Herbie Goes to Monte Carlo*, with him. He had watched it a half dozen times so he knew this line from Don Knotts well and knew when to use it.

I didn't do much traveling as it took most of my time figuring out the proper office protocol and getting my staff settled. In August Joyce accompanied me to Nigeria where we held a teacher's conference for 3,000 teachers from all over the country. One of our memorable experiences was at a small airport at Aba. We were taking in wheelchairs for two handicapped young people and the customs official at Aba decided he wanted them. They held our luggage until everyone else had left the airport and then they put a chain on the doors and locked us in. They proceeded to take our suitcases into a back room and make us open them. They started going through them with an eye on the wheelchairs. They knew if they could confiscate them, then they could sell them for big money. Our host, Moses Umoh, finally showed up with our passports after clearing them with immigration. To say that Moses was upset would be putting it mildly. He verbally dressed the guy up one side and down the other. We were let go without further incident with the wheelchairs intact.

On September 9, 1997, Samuel Avraham was born in Boston. If I recall correctly, I was at an ACSI convention. Carl McGarvey from the C&MA was visiting Jeff and Michaela to do their interview for Africa. Joyce was aware that Michaela was going into labor, so she got a flight from Colorado Springs and arrived in Boston only to find out that Samuel had been born a few minutes before. Before Joyce had a chance to see him, a nurse came in to say that they had taken him to NICU. This was a precautionary measure because he had birth fluid in his lungs. It was a scary time for everyone. This meant he had to stay extra time in the hospital. By the time I got to Boston, Michaela was home with her firstborn son. Joyce stayed for a week to help Michaela get adjusted to having a baby to care for.

In October we had a wonderful visit from both girls and four grandchildren. Samuel was just six weeks old when he made his first trip to visit Papa and Beba in Colorado Springs. Melissa brought Michael, Brandon and Michelle so they could all see the newest addition to the family. While they were there, we got a major Albuquerque low snowstorm that dumped 23 inches of snow on Colorado Springs. Michaela was to fly back to Boston the next day but was delayed a day because the airport was closed. It was just the first of many snows for Samuel.

Refugee Rescue

Shortly after our move to Colorado Springs, Joyce received a letter from Cote de Ivoire from a pastor in a refugee camp. Rev. Cheiwlu (Chei) Bargboe had met a missionary who had an old ACSI directory. He was writing to inquire about membership in ACSI for a high school he had started in a UN refugee camp. He had a deep longing and burden for these young people who were without an opportunity for an education. He and his family, along with several others, had fled the ethnic cleansing that was taking place in Liberia. They fled as their home was being torched by the rebels. They hid in the bushes by day and traveled by night. Their first-born son was a toddler and their second born was just hours old when they fled. The mother, Grace, carried him in a plastic tub.

Chei had started Christ the King Lutheran School under a tree. They had no money for buildings. Even though Joyce told him by return mail that she would find someone to pay their membership fee, he still sent a letter with 17 one-dollar bills to pay toward his membership. We were able to contact the International Christian Academy (ICA) in Bouake and Evan and Jewel Evans organized a student outreach group that traveled to the camp to build a classroom building for them. They also took school supplies for the students.

Due to the civil war that spread across the border from Liberia, the refugee camp closed and they had to flee for their lives once again. They fled as far as Ghana, where they found a small house for shelter. Joyce and I paid their monthly rent and sent money for food. In one of their return letters, they told how during a gap when we were unable to get money to them, they were down to one cup of rice. Chei wrote, "my wife Grace cooked the last cup of rice for the family on July 26. Yet not a day has closed without the Lord providing a cup of rice for the kids. Praise His name." This was another one of those faith-building miracles of God's provision and praising Jehovah Jira my provider.

While in Ghana, they were advised by the UN that they needed to return to Cote de Ivoire and register if they were to have a chance of being resettled outside of Cote de Ivoire. They went to Abidjan and the only place

they could find to live was in a slum area where the living conditions were squalid. They all ended up with Cholera. The only way they could see a doctor to get medicine was to pay upfront, so we sent them more money so they could get the medical attention they needed.

They were finally approved to leave the country if they had a government approved sponsor, all the appropriate documentation and the backing for their airline tickets. *Now folks, we're talking 11 people here!* Joyce and I had been praying about what to do. We felt surly that God hadn't brought them this far to let them down. *"Our God is a God who saves; from the Sovereign Lord comes escape from death."* Psalm 68:20 NIV We were working with Teresa Towes in Winnipeg, Canada. Teresa is Henry Towes daughter in law, who was able to get her church in Winnipeg to be the sponsoring church and government approval.

I was having lunch in Colorado Springs with a dear friend Arnie Trillet who casually asked me what was on my heart. That seemed like a strange question to be asked out of the blue. But then God does work in mysterious ways his wonders to perform. We hadn't shared our involvement with the Bargeboe family previously. I told him their story and mentioned everything was in place for them to be received in Canada except the funding for their airline tickets. The next day I got a call from Arnie to say that their airline tickets would be covered. God had showed up in a big way, HIS FAITHFULNESS never ceases to amaze us. They arrived in Canada just before Christmas. Immigration officials in Toronto met them in the airport with winter coats, mittens and boots. They arrived in Winnipeg to a fully furnished home and a warm reception by the people of the church. Sometime later, Joyce and I had the privilege of going to Winnipeg to meet them and participate in a Sunday service where Chei shared their story. One of their girls is named after Joyce.

I was remarkably busy during 1998. I traveled to the Philippines and Joyce went with me on trips to Guatemala and a survey trip to the Middle East to visit struggling Christian schools.

In addition to all this madness of travel, we also made a trip to that foreign country of Alabama for a wedding in Tuscaloosa. Matthew and Melei tied the knot on August 15. I can't believe that I was able to fly in and still do their flowers. Marshall and Elizabeth had moved to her mom and dad's so their little house in Alberta City was empty. We cranked down the air and brought in the flowers. It all came off well for a makeshift flower shop. We were surprised when we found out that Melei wore cowgirl boots under her wedding dress. They were off to Mexico for a honeymoon trip.

The Middle East

At the beginning of September, Joyce and I flew to the Middle East for an ACSI survey trip to struggling Christian schools. However, our first stop was Israel, where we spent a week with Jeff, Michaela and Samuel. They were there while Jeff was immersing himself in modern Hebrew. Jeff was our tour guide for a whirlwind trip around Israel. It was incredible to visit the places where Jesus and his disciples had walked. We would visit during the day and then go back to the C&MA guest house at night and open our Bibles to the biblical account of the day's events. We spent a night at a Kibbutz on the Sea of Galilee. Samuel had a great time sitting in the water throwing stones into the sea. We also made a visit to the Dead Sea where we experienced the weightlessness of floating in the dense salt and mineral water. At some point on the journey, we made it to the top of Masada where the temperatures seemed to bake you. Samuel wouldn't keep his hat on to protect him from the sun as he sat in his carrier on Jeff's back. Other places included the Mount of Olives, the old city of Jerusalem, Ein Gedi, Caesarea, Jericho and a host of other places too numerous to mention. We had a short trip into Ramallah to visit with Ann and Louis Ziglar, close friends from Nyack We were ushered into their apartment building under armed guard. Israel and the Palestinians were at war in the Gaza Strip. It's hard to pick a favorite place since all of Israel is so special.

One special event during our week in Israel was the celebration of Samuel's first birthday. He had an idiosyncrasy, could have been from the heat on Masada, where he would take his toys, throw them over his shoulder, then turn around and throw them over his shoulder again. Weird!! This one-year-old and I also got a historical or hysterical ride on a camel in Jericho.

I had specifically asked the immigration agent when we entered Israel not to stamp our passports because we knew it would keep us from entering Lebanon. When we were getting ready to leave Israel, we discovered they had stamped Joyce's passport. When we got to Egypt, we had to spend about a half day getting new passport photos and then going to the US Embassy to get Joyce a new passport.

We visited a couple of Christian schools in Cairo. It was strange to walk up to an unmarked gate and high wall and enter to find a school in a large house. They had to be very secretive because of the Muslim faith and legal requirements. So, no signs. We did get a short tour of Cairo from Faith Kenoyer, one of the school principals. She took us to visit the pyramids and the Sphinx. The traffic in Cairo was absolutely mind blowing! You take your life in your own hands when you get behind the wheel.

Our next stop was Amman, Jordan. When we arrived and while we were waiting for our ride, I decided to go to an upper level of the airport to confirm our departure date and our tickets. Joyce was going to wait for our hosts. She asked me how she would know them when they arrived. Duh! Every woman in the airport had on a black burka with little slits for their eyes and lots of gold bracelets. I said "Joyce, look around. I think it will be someone dressed like us." We spent about three days and visited the Whitman Academy, a school for MKs and Internationals. I met with the board of the school and the Director. We saw some of the most incredible Roman ruins, probably the most complete standing columns that we had seen anywhere.

Next stop was Beirut, Lebanon where we met with a school director who wanted his school to become a member of ACSI. However, we learned the school was not a Christian school, only a school with a weak Christian ethos. On our drive from the airport to the school, we couldn't believe our eyes at the bombed-out buildings as we snaked our way through the city and up over the mountains to the Bekaa Valley. The school was out in the Bekaa Valley not far from the Israeli border. We could hear the bombs and rockets exploding as they were very much at war. Some of the school buildings had pock marks where it had been shelled. When we traveled from the airport, we went through a lot of Syrian checkpoints as Lebanon was still occupied by Syria. There was one whole section of the trip where we went through village after village that were totally abandoned. These were the villages where Druze Christians had lived who fled the area because of persecution.

We were near the mountains where the Cedars of Lebanon grew. Our host took us to see the forest where it is likely that Nehemiah got the timber to rebuild the gates of Jerusalem. It is also possible that the trees that are there now were seedlings when Nehemiah secured the timber from the keeper of the King's Forest. It was quite an inspirational trip. Our whole

Middle East encounter will always stand out in our memory as one of our favorites because of its significance in biblical history and prophecy.

I would return to Lebanon a couple more times to work with the school and provide professional development for the teachers. The school was under the direction of a new headmaster who was pushing for the school to become more Christian in its ethos. On one of those trips, I was taken to visit a well-preserved Roman ruin, a temple to honor one of the Caesars. On the same site was a temple to Baccas, the goddess of wine, and a temple to Baal. It was like, "Pick a god; if one doesn't work for you, try another

Our Alabama Family

After our move to Colorado, my mom was left all alone. Steve and Diane were home for furlough in 1999, and she lived with them in Birmingham for the year. She was becoming frail and didn't need to be alone in the home where she and dad had lived in Northport. We sold her house in Northport and Steve rented a U-Haul truck and he and mom headed out across country for Colorado Springs. We had secured a place for her in a senior care facility where she would have her own apartment. She was adamant that she didn't want to live with us because she said our lives were too busy and when we were gone, she would be left alone. She was wise because I was all over the world that year. 1999 was a bit of a blur for me. It was a heavy year of travel from South Africa to Paraguay to the Philippines and several ACSI conventions in between.

On November 16, whippersnapper #5 was born to Jeff and Michaela. Elijah Aharon was born in a Boston hospital. Joyce flew from Colorado Springs to Boston and got there the day after he was born. I was speaking at an ACSI convention and was able to rearrange my ticket to make a stopover in Boston. Michaela was greatly surprised. I even think I saw a few tears.

Marshall and Elizabeth built a new house in Coaling, Alabama so Marshall would be closer to his work at McWayne in Birmingham. Elizabeth was teaching at County High and heavily involved in drama productions.

In 2000 Joyce traveled with me to South Africa on two occasions. ACSI sponsored a first South Africa Christian Educators Conference at the

Hatfield church and school in Pretoria. We stayed at a beautiful B & B on a game farm with all sorts of wild animals. The first trip was to meet with the planning committee to prepare for the conference. That same year we both traveled to Hawaii for staff meetings that included our international staff. What an exotic and enchanted place. In October I traveled to the Philippines and opened the ACSI office under the leadership of Steve and Kay Abelman.

A Matriarch Passes

We were facing another sad year for our family as mom, Martha Virginia Brock Renicks passed on March 14, 2001. When I got the news, I was in South Africa with Ken Smitherman, my boss, interviewing candidates for the directorship of the newly established ACSI South Africa office. Joyce was the one they notified that mom was in a coma and was taken to Penrose Main Hospital. I was shocked when I got the news and it was an absolute scramble to get a flight out of Johannesburg that same night. Jill Battle, the office secretary, got me on a Virgin Atlantic flight to London and a United Airlines flight to Denver. The staff of both airlines were most sympathetic and helpful, ushering me through back channels of security at London Heathrow airport. Both airlines gave me business class seats.

Steve was in Brazil and had to make similar arrangements to get home. Mom was still in a coma and the hospital had put her on a ventilator. I sat and sang hymns and read scripture to her. She died while on the ventilator and while Steve was still in route from the Colorado Springs airport to the hospital.

Once Steve got there, we arranged with a local funeral home to prepare her for transport to Ohio where we would hold her memorial service. Doug

Dry, our pastor at the C&MA Church in Colorado Springs, was to officiate the service. Joyce, Steve and I flew to Columbus and mom's casket was on the same flight with us. The last flight we would all take together. A memorial service was held at the Zanesville C&MA Church. As people were given an opportunity to speak, the remark most often heard was that mom was a servant. Most of her family were able to attend.

Our Dreams

In August Joyce and I flew to South Africa for the dedication of the new ACSI office. We cut the ribbon. Following the dedication, the staff of ACSI treated us to a safari in the Kruger Park. A scene that is etched in my mind is a large herd of elephants showering and bathing themselves in the river. There was also a troop of baboons, dozens of them, sleeping in a tree in the heat of mid-day. We stayed in little bungalows with a thatched roof. It was a great bonding time with the new South Africa staff. We had commissioned Alan Sutherland and Samson Makhado at the conference as director and associate director. They along with their wives Anita and Mavis respectfully, Ian Vermooten, Tony and Arlene Selby and Jill Battle accompanied us on the Safari.

One of my great burdens and heartbeats was for the multitude of vulnerable children at risk in South Africa. There were so many children that were languishing in every community.

> *"Arise, cry out in the night, as the watches of the night begin; pour out your heart like water in the presence of the Lord. Lift up your hands to him for the lives of your children, who are faint from hunger at every street corner."* Lamentations 2:19 NIV

In 2002, Alan McIlhenny and I became good friends and partnered together to hold a task force on children at risk in South Africa. Out of this task force, Alan and I co-founded Open Schools Worldwide (OSWW). Our response to the children languishing in the villages and informal settlements (slums) not only of Africa but around the world. It was my dream to see these vulnerable children have a hope and a future. As of this writing 2021 OSWW is serving thousands of vulnerable children in South Africa, Zambia, Zimbabwe, Malawi, Kenya, Ethiopia and preparing to startup new sites in Ghana Uganda and Brazil. Our dream is on its way to being fulfilled.

Michael with sponsored kids Guatemala

One of the dreams that Joyce and I had was to take our grandchildren with us to an overseas location to show them the work that we did. This was the year, 2003, and we took our firstborn grandson Michael. We planned a trip for him to Guatemala since he and the Jean family had been sponsoring two children through the ACSI sponsorship program. We were able to visit with both sponsored children in their homes. Michael took Christmas presents for each of them. We also visited the Christian school where they attended. Every Latin American city has a central plaza with a large Catholic church at the heart of it and usually with fountains and government buildings. Michael visited interesting sights in and around the central plaza and the central market. Michael learned to bargain for prices on gifts for his family and friends. Of course, I was there looking over his shoulder to make sure he wasn't being taken advantage of. We also took him to our favorite place in Guatemala, the city of Antigua. No trip to Guatemala would be complete without a trip to Lake Atitlan. At the end of our time in Guatemala Michael's observation was, "Now I know how to better pray for my sponsored friends."

New Additions

We added whippersnapper number six in 2003. Brock Matthew was born on a beautiful day, October 21st. I had stayed in Tuscaloosa a whole week in their camper waiting for this new baby, but he didn't arrive on the scene before I had to leave for an overseas trip. Matthew and Melei were building a new house in Coaling near Marshall and Elizabeth. Matthew kept delaying the move because all the finishing touches were not complete. Joyce came to help Melei with Brock. Melei was anxious to get moved and settled, so Joyce and Michaela loaded up many of the already packed boxes and started the move. I think that got Matthew motivated to complete the move. Matthew had gone into business with his two brothers in law and purchased Spanky's portable toilet business. Melei was working at Rise as a teacher/helper.

Jeff and Michaela moved back to Birmingham to the basement apartment at Jeff's mom and dads. Jeff took a job at Briarwood Christian High School teaching Bible and Michaela worked remotely doing the billing for Dr. Rosenthal. A few years later, Jeff got a professorship at Samford University and Michaela became a teacher in the transitional kindergarten at Briarwood Christian Elementary School.

Another Matriarch Passes

Standing at the threshold of 2004, unbeknown to us, we were facing a full and busy year and a sad one. Joyce's mom, Margaret Ellen McCray Armitage, had been quite ill for several months and continued to go downhill. On March 11, she took her last breath on earth and flew into the arms of Jesus whom she loved and had served faithfully. Our entire family was able to make it to Butler for her memorial service and burial. I had flown in from overseas and didn't have a clean white shirt or tie. I stopped in a shop at the Pittsburgh airport and bought them.

We were all saddened but were relieved that she didn't have to suffer any longer. All four of the Armitage kids spoke and shared memories of their mom. It was a very uplifting service. She was buried next to Joyce's dad at East Branch Cemetery near Cobbs Corners. Following the graveside service, we took our four and their families all around the area to show them where Joyce grew up.

More Adventures and Sadness

It was time for Brandon to take his trip with us overseas. We took him to an ACSI conference in Vienna, Austria in April 2004. He was introduced to the work of ACSI around the world through the lens of International Christian schools. We did some sightseeing in Vienna, which took in a medieval castle high above the Danube River, where he got to hold a falcon. While in Vienna, he got to see a performance of the Lipizzaner Stallions. Following the conference, we took the train to Budapest where we stayed at the ACSI office and guest house. We took the bus in and out of the city and visited the sights of Budapest from the central historic district to Gilllert Hill.

This trip was a difficult and sad one for me. My best friend and colleague, Dave Pollock, had fallen ill while in Vienna prior to the conference. He was one of the featured speakers, so this left a major hole in the conference program. It also left a huge hole in my heart. Dave slipped into a coma and never recovered. I stayed by his bedside for several hours reading scripture, singing hymns and praying. His wife Betty Lou, daughter Michelle, and sons Mike and Daniel made their way to Budapest as quickly as possible. I stood by Dave's bedside with them while they grieved, and I grieved with them. It put a damper on the rest of our trip.

Dave and I were as close as any two brothers. We spent a lot of time together on various ministry trips and we visited each other in our respective homes. We often spent significant time in prayer for each other's families, shared our dreams and visions for future ministry and together we launched several initiatives all aimed at how mission organizations, international schools and missionary parents were tasked to nurture MKs and plan for MK care.

World Champions

In July Joyce and I drove from Colorado Springs to Kansas City to watch Michael and the team from Franklin play in the 11-year-old World Series. If our memory isn't too faulty, I think there were 96 teams from across the US. Much to our surprise, Michael's team, the Mustangs, kept winning and finally won it all in the finals. There was great cheering and backslapping.

We painted our Trooper with white shoe polish: "World Champs' 'Congratulations Michael." We headed back to Colorado Springs with Melissa and her three kids. We were thrilled that Michaela, Samuel and Elijah were flying into Colorado Springs the following day. We spent the next week doing all kinds of fun stuff. I took the kids and went miniature golfing. It was one of the highlights next to Garden of the Gods and the Flying W Ranch. We also took them to Focus on the Family where they enjoyed the kids' zone and especially the three-story slide. The only trouble was that Elijah was not tall enough to go on the slide and he kept saying, "But I be bigger." We enjoyed the hot tub on our back deck in the cool of the evenings.

Surgery and Sadness

In September I had double knee replacement surgery. Dr. O'Bryan was my surgeon and the orthopedic surgeon for the U.S. Olympic team. The U.S. Olympic village was in Colorado Springs. Matthew came out to be with Joyce during my surgery. The night after I had the surgery, I had lost a lot of blood. I was awake and talking to Matthew when I started talking out of my head and then lost consciousness. At that point there was a mad scramble of the nurses and finally a head nurse came and decided that I needed a blood transfusion. Altogether, during and after surgery, I had lost a total of four pints of blood. Prior to surgery, I had given two pints of my own blood to use in case I needed it. Following a short stay in the hospital, with Matthew staying all night with me, I was transferred to a rehab hospital where I spent 11 days in excruciating pain. But at the end I was able to walk out with just a cane. After I went home, Melissa came out to be with me during the day while Joyce worked. She took me to outpatient rehab three times a week. She was an incredibly good nurse and a great encouragement.

We flew to Alabama for Christmas to be with the family. The sadness and grief were not over. The day after Christmas we got a call from Debbie Solari, Joyce's younger sister, to say that her husband Mike had died while driving home from the gym where he ran every day. He was driving up the Mercer Street hill. He had a massive heart attack and crashed into a large boulder in the yard of a home. Using some of my air miles we flew to Pittsburgh for the memorial service and burial. We flew back to Nashville and all the kids came so we could have Christmas together. 2004 is not a year we wanted to repeat.

2005 was a much happier year. We welcomed two more whippersnappers, numbers seven and eight to the family. On March 1, William Hamlet (Will) was born. This was a time of great joy. Marshall and Elizabeth had waited and hoped and prayed for a child for 14 years. Everyone in the family was ecstatic. Elizabeth decided to quit teaching at County High and become a stay-at-home mom. When Will was old enough for school, she decided to home school and she also held a leadership role in Classical Conversation, a home-schooling consortium. Marshall continued to work at DESHAZO Crane in Alabaster, Alabama as the lead engineer.

On July 16 we welcomed Cason Stephen. Mathew and Melei were keeping up the tradition of two Renicks boys per family. This pattern started in a prior generation with my grandfather William and his brother Samuel. Then in my dad's family it was my dad and his brother Wilfred. My mom and dad had two boys, Philip and Stephen. We had two boys, Marshall and Matthew. Steve had two boys, Tim and Paul, and all our children had two boys. Marshall and Elizabeth still had one to come.

A Cruise of a Lifetime

September of 2005 Joyce and I flew to Athens, Greece and met our friends Alan and Malinda Brown for a cruise in the Greek Isles. This trip was a delayed 40th Anniversary celebration for us and the 40th for Alan and Melinda. Before the cruise we did some sightseeing around Athens. One of the highlights for me was a hike to the top of the Acropolis from our hotel. It had been one year to the day that I had my knee surgery.

We boarded our Greek cruise ship, the Aegean I, bound for the beautiful Greek Isles. Our first stop was Mykonos. It was a beautiful afternoon and a beautiful island with gleaming white buildings, windmills and narrow streets with bright colored bougainvillea. As we boarded the ship to leave, the sun was setting and it gave us a glorious send off. We also visited the islands of Crete, Rhodes, Patmos, Santorini and the city of Ephesus in Turkey.

Our time in Ephesus gave us a feeling of awe as we walked the streets where the Apostle Paul had walked and stood in the amphitheater where

Paul addressed the Ephesians. The amphitheater was incredible. Built by the Romans, you could stand at the front of the amphitheater and speak in a normal voice and be heard at the very top row. They were some engineers. We also visited a beautiful wool and cashmere market. Very pricy.

> *I, John, … was exiled to the island of Patmos for preaching the word of God and for my testimony about Jesus.* Revelation 1:9 NLT

On the Island of Patmos, we visited the Cave of the Apocalypse where it is believed that the Apostle John received and wrote the book of Revelation. He had been exiled there by the Romans. There was a feeling of awe and reverence standing there in the cave where he slept and wrote. While on the cross, Jesus charged John to care for his mother Mary, so it is likely that she lived for periods of time on the Island. She also lived in Ephesus from time to time.

Santorini was the last island on the tour so we decided to disembark the ship at Santorini. We had booked a hotel for three nights so we could explore this most beautiful of all the islands. Our hotel was down the side of the island, 68 steps from the street level. Our room was in a cave overlooking the Caldera, very romantic. There were beautiful sunsets as we sat on the patio of our hotel by the pool sharing a glass of wine. We loved looking out over the brilliant blue domes and the iridescent blue waters of the Mediterranean Sea. Santorini is probably number one on our list of the most beautiful places in the world that we have ever visited. We had pre-booked flights from Santorini to Athens, where we boarded flights to home. A trip we will never forget.

2006 was a year of hunkering down and getting things at ACSI consolidated so we could retire in 2007. I was also working hard on preparations for the first all Africa Roundtable to be held in Johannesburg. I made a trip to JoBerg to meet with the planning team headed by Angie Pape and select the venue.

Our last Christmas in Colorado didn't disappoint. Marshall, Elizabeth and the boys, as well as Matthew, Melei and their kids, came for the holidays. We had a real honest to goodness snowstorm. Matthew and Melei were delayed getting there and the Denver airport was wall to wall people who were stranded and couldn't get out. We had a beautiful white Christmas and everyone enjoyed sledding down the hill in front of our house. Will stood on the sidewalk and cried watching Marshall and Elizabeth come down on the sled together. We took a day trip to Breckenridge.

In March 2007, I travelled to South Africa for the first All Africa Round Table. I went early to get things set up for the conference. 200 delegates traveled from countries across Africa to participate. It was an exciting time for all. All sessions were held in an auditorium that was tiered and set up like the United Nations. Each table had its own mike and flag of the country represented by the delegate. Delegates could push a button on their microphone to be acknowledged. All sessions were simultaneously translated to French. Delegates came from every African nation, with the exceptions of Mauritania, Algeria and Libya.

Joyce her sister Debbie, and JuLee Davis Meecham, came a few days later due to a stopover in Amsterdam for a day of sightseeing. They did the canal boat tour and a hop on hop off bus tour. They saw the Anne Frank house. Debbie was blown away with the mix of people at the Round Table and loved getting to know them. The Round Table more than fulfilled my expectations and set the direction for ACSI in Africa. The impact is still being felt.

Following the Round Table, we took some vacation days. Joyce, Debbie and I flew to Cape Town and stayed in a little cottage that was a bed and breakfast. We had breakfast in the main house and after breakfast we did a lot of touring around the Cape Town area. Jeanne Westgate, a friend, was our tour guide. Unfortunately, the cable car to the top of Table Mountain wasn't running because of high winds. I think it's because Joyce and Debbie didn't want to go and prayed that it wouldn't run. We went to the Cape of Good Hope on a windy blustery day.

Another friend of ours Karen Cerff had a cottage in Hermanus along the Indian Ocean coast. She was gracious to let us use it for a few days. We did some sightseeing and whale watching. We walked across a long beach over big sand dunes to get to the water. The water was freezing cold. On the way back to Cape Town to catch our flight home we drove along the Garden Route and stopped at some vineyards for wine tasting.

Retirement Years – Time for a Retread

Sadly, when we returned home, it was time to get the house at 1097 Golden Hills Rd. ready to put on the market for sale. In May we put the house on the market, and we signed the sale papers on July 3rd. During this time, we put a down payment on a house in Franklin, Tennessee. At the International Staff meetings in July, the International Staff held a party for us at the Sunbird Restaurant overlooking the city of Colorado Springs. At the global staff meetings that included all the North American directors we were treated to a world premiere screening of a video of our lives and ministry at ACSI. JuLee had even traveled to Alabama to interview our kids.

As I traveled to the various international regions of ACSI, I was given warm welcomes, farewell dinners and mementos and a send-off from the staff of the regional offices. Probably the most memorable was the one in South Africa. I had invested a lot of time and myself in that region in developing leaders from the Regional Director, Samson Makhado, to individual headmasters and directors of schools. Prior to the Round Table, Tony Selby, headmaster of the King's School, Robin Hills, hosted my retirement party. The cooking class of the school prepared and served a professional five-star meal. The entertainment was a gospel quartet called "Imagine", a group I had fallen in love with a couple years prior. Several school directors/headmasters, ACSI staff and former staff, teachers and friends were in attendance. The big surprise of the evening was the presentation of a large, beautiful painting of the *Lion of Judah* that they shipped to Franklin for us.

We retired on the last day of July and the closing on our Colorado house was the second week of August. The movers loaded us up and we were on the road headed for Franklin, Tennessee. Joyce and I drove the Rodeo. We took the southern route through New Mexico and Texas. We took two days for the drive. Although it was exciting to think that we were going to be closer to our family, it was hard to leave all our friends at ACSI and the friends that we had made in Colorado Springs. We will always miss the mountains! It was a very emotional time for us. Time to retread. Melissa had started teaching again at Christ Presbyterian Academy. Brent continued his position as a CPA for one of the health consortiums in Brentwood/Nashville.

Although we were retired from ACSI, we stayed engaged in ministry. In October after we had settled in Franklin, Joyce and I had been invited to Morrison Academy in Taiwan. I led the board in sessions on "scenario planning." We encountered our first typhoon while we were there. Tim and Bonnie McGill, and the staff of Morrison Academy treated us like royalty. They sent us off across the island to a beautiful gorge and waterfalls for several days and lavished us with gifts.

After a year, I decided I had sat still long enough, so I started volunteering at African Leadership in 2008. I had known Larry Warren, Executive Director of African Leadership, from attending Christ Community Church with Melissa and Brent. I started volunteering to help them with some education-related projects in Kenya and Malawi. Shortly after that, they offered me a part-time job when they realized what a valuable resource I was. They sent me to Kenya to check out the project at New Dawn High School and then to Malawi to look over the beginnings of a school called Adziwa (He Knows). The duration of my time at African Leadership lasted until after we moved to Alabama in 2013. This time involved many trips to Africa, and the building a beautiful container school building in Nairobi, Kenya at New Dawn. It was built from 8 high cube containers. The dedication was in August 2012. My recommendations for Adziwa included the building of several classroom buildings to expand the school in Lilongwe, Malawi. I also did a lot of professional development for the staff of both schools.

Great Family Travels and Blessings

God blessed Marshall and Elizabeth with another son. We were excited to welcome whippersnapper number nine, Jackson Marshall, on March 11, 2008. Joyce came from Franklin to help Elizabeth take care of Jackson.

Joyce and I traveled to Budapest for the 15th anniversary celebration of the beginning of ACSI Eastern Europe. We used this occasion to take Michelle on her trip. We stopped in Paris on the way to help fulfill Michelle's dream of seeing as many Monet paintings as she could. She dragged us all over the city to the Louvre Museum of Art, the Monet Museum, the Eiffel

Tower, Notre Dame Cathedral and a boat tour of Paris along the Seine. From Paris we flew to Budapest.

We did a lot of sightseeing and toured all the special places in and around Budapest. We went to Fishermen's Bastion that gives a bird's eye view of the city that is split between Buda and Pest by the Danube River. We walked the streets of the old city, visited Heroes Square, Gillert Hill and traveled to the town of Szentendre Village Museum. Michelle sat in the central square for a caricature portrait to take home to her dad and mom.

Joyce and I celebrated our 45th wedding anniversary in Las Vegas. We had traded one of our Westgate timeshare weeks for a week in Las Vegas. We did some touring around and were enjoying the engineering marvel of Hoover Dam when we got a call from Dale telling us that Joyce's brother

Ron had passed at his own hand. We drove out into the desert so we could get a decent cell signal and I spent considerable time on the phone with Delta rebooking our flights. Since this turned out to be our last night in Las Vegas, with saddened hearts, we went to see the stage play Momma Mia that lifted our spirits.

We flew to Nashville to repack and head to Pittsburgh. Matthew flew in from Birmingham and we picked him

Ron Armitage
1948 - 2008

up in Pittsburgh to drive to Butler. We were shocked at Ron's death but not totally surprised after a long battle with bi-polar disorder. During visiting hours at the funeral home, we were surprised at the number of people who came to pay their respects. Many of them were indigent and from the homeless population of Butler. They told many stories of how Ron looked after them. The police chief told us that he didn't know what he was going to do without Ron, because Ron was the only one who knew where the homeless stayed. We had no idea the breadth of Ron's ministry or how well loved he was. Ron had been living in the house that belonged to Joyce's mom. Joyce and I stayed after the funeral to help her sisters and brother clean out the house and get it ready to sell.

Michaela and Jeff bought a house in Indian Springs so we helped them prep and paint so they could get moved in. The worst was trying to remove all the old wallpaper. I went to help paint, but Jeff's dad was sure I couldn't do it well enough to please him. Never mind that I had painted for a contractor when I was teaching school. It had been a great summer job for me. Side note: I passed the Leonard test and helped paint.

In 2009 we hit the jackpot. We were thrilled at the birth of another granddaughter; Ava Marie was born to Matthew and Melei on February 18th. She was a little bundle of joy and her brothers were so proud of her. Joyce came down from Franklin to do what she does best, take care of grandbabies. Matthew was in the process of getting them settled in the house in Woodland Hills. It's a good thing they didn't have any more kids or they would have moved again.

Within a few months of Ava's birth Melei noticed spots on Ava's skin that looked like birthmarks. With her background of working with special needs students she made an appointment with their pediatrician to confirm her suspicions. It was confirmed that Ava had neurofibromatosis. This has been a constant reminder to pray that she didn't develop tumors that attack the nerves. She had a lot of weakness in her left leg and had to wear a brace to protect this very active little girl's leg from breaking.

Whippersnapper Camp

We started having the three little boys, Brock, Will and Carson, come to Franklin for a week at a time so we could spend more time with them. The first year wasn't without tears of homesickness. We loaded them and all their gear in the car and off we went to Franklin. On the drive from Tuscaloosa, we did all kinds of silly things. We told stories where one person, usually me or Joyce, would start with a line then someone would add a line to it. Being little boys, the stories always seemed to end with monsters.

When I stopped for gas and before I realized it, all three of them were out of their seats and running across the fuel plaza on their way in the door of a McDonalds. I didn't even realize it was there. The Golden Arches were calling.

This soon became known as *Whippersnapper Camp*. We planned all kinds of things to occupy them. We went to the Nashville Zoo, the Nashville Science Center, to the creek at the park where they loved to play, we went swimming at our neighborhood pool and at Prairie Life. Joyce always had a Bible time with them each morning and crafts. We had various helpers, Michelle, Michaela and Elijah.

When we moved to Alabama in 2013, we continued to have the camp at our house and backyard. By now, Ava and Jackson had joined the group. They slept outside in a tent where Elijah entertained them with weird stories. We had sack races, soap carving, kayaking, swimming, fishing tournaments (boring) and even some boy scout knot tying. These are memories that Joyce and I will always treasure. We hope they do, too. Each of you should write your own memories of whippersnapper camp.

Joyce started volunteering with William Mwizerwa in 2010 at what would become Legacy Mission Village, a ministry to refugee families in Nashville. She started a pre-school program on a shoestring. The aim was to get these children, many of whom had no English at all, ready to go to kindergarten in the public school system. She was everywhere and at any garage sale she could find looking for furniture and playthings for the children. She started the program with 11 kids and grew it to 20. It's now 2021 and the program has continued.

Travels and Celebrations

In April 2010 we celebrated the 20th year of the opening of the first office of ACSI in Guatemala. Joyce and I were invited to be part of the celebration. I had the opportunity to recount God's FAITHFULNESS over the 20 years and to thank Stuart, Sheny and the staff for their dedication in growing the Christian School movement throughout Latin America.

Samuel participating in an Open Schools event with
students from Eagles Nest Christian School

In May we took Samuel to South Africa. We wanted him to experience a different world than what he was growing up in. In Johannesburg, we stayed in a B&B and met Anna Marie Russell, ACSI South Africa Director, who took us to visit various projects, including an orphanage that was conducting an OSWW program. One of the little girls sat on Joyce's lap and begged to go home with her. Samuel was quite popular with the kids since he had taken candy and balloons for them. This was a stop on our way to Eagle's Nest Christian School, where we stayed in the guest house hosted by Mac and Elsa Vandenberg. Samuel was put on the spot in that he had to speak to the high school students following a very flowery prepared speech by the head of student government welcoming him to South Africa.

We took Samuel to the village of Nobody with a student group from Eagle's Nest that was running an afterschool OSWW program. This was quite an eye-opener for all of us to see kids who were from upper elementary to high school that were just learning to read and write.

Mac and Elsa, to show appreciation to us for coming, took us on an overnight Safari to the Kruger Park. Samuel was so keen to see all the animals. There were a lot of elephants, giraffe, lion and baboons. We did get to see all the big five, including a white rhino. We capped off our visit to the lion park just outside of Joburg where Samuel got to hold a baby lion. We had gone for pizza at lunch and had put the leftovers in the trunk (boot) of the car. Samuel was concerned before we entered the park that the lions would smell the pizza. We assured him that lions didn't like pizza because they were meat eaters. Sure enough, they began following our car around the park, climbed up on the back of the car and tried to eat the taillight. It was exciting at first, then it started to get scary as the lions got more and more aggressive.

This was the year of the World Cup of soccer. South Africa was hosting the games, so Anna Marie Russell had met us at the airport with a vuvuzela horn used to make as much noise as possible at a soccer match. We got to see two of the new stadiums built for this special occasion in South Africa.

Michael graduated from high school in 2011, with honors from Christ Presbyterian Academy. The school gives a graduating senior who has shown exceptional leadership and achievement in all areas of learning and citizenship at the highest level of Christian character an award called Soli de Gloria. Michael was the recipient. We were all so proud of him. That fall Michael went off to Mississippi State University to begin his university career.

I continued to work for African Leadership and traveled to Africa especially in finishing up the building of the resource center at New Dawn.

Elijah was next in line for an overseas trip. I had been invited as the guest speaker at an administrator conference in the Dominican Republic. With Elijah in tow, we flew to Santo Domingo. We arrived on the eve of Elijah's birthday. We were staying in a private home of a friend of Lester Flaquer, headmaster of the Santo Domingo Christian Academy and ACSI Director for the Caribbean in Santo Domingo. That night Marta, our hostess, took us to the Hilton Hotel for a fine dinner and in celebration of Elijah's birthday she had ordered a cake and party favors.

The following morning at breakfast, Elijah's real birthday, he had a special breakfast and then another cake with 12 candles. What a way to celebrate your birthday. We took Elijah to Santo Domingo Christian Academy with Lester. What we didn't know was that the 6th grade class had planned yet another birthday party for him. All the girls had eyes for Elijah.

Elijah with a new friend at the mission school.

I went with Lester to the administrator conference and Joyce and Elijah went on two-and-a-half-hour drive into the countryside to a small mission school located on a farm that was run by an older missionary couple. Elijah immediately got involved with some of the students and spent the day with them. He visited classes and then got a tour of the farm and the village where the kids lived. They drove by a training camp for baseball, knowing that many of the best baseball players in US major league baseball come from the Dominican.

When I was reunited with Joyce and Elijah, our hostess Marta had secured box seat tickets to a local farm team baseball game. She had gotten

Elijah a baseball cap, a signed baseball and a horn for making noise. She did it up big to try and show Elijah a good time.

Lester and his wife took us to a beach where we stayed right on the beach in a condo that belonged to his brother. It had a beautiful pool. The water in the Caribbean was very shallow and you could walk out for a long way. There was a restaurant at the end of a long board walk type pier where we ate.

Joyce, Elijah and I toured the historic area of Santo Domingo and visited all the places where Christopher Columbus had lived while visiting the island. We did all of this on foot in the rain. We went to the Hard Rock Café for lunch and then Elijah did some shopping for gifts and souvenirs before we headed home.

Fulfillment of a Dream

For me, 2012 was a significant year in the culmination of a multi-year project at New Dawn Christian School in Kenya. The school is in the informal settlement of Huruma. The new resource center, which started because of my evaluation of the school in 2009, was finally finished and the dedication was scheduled for August 10. Joyce and I, along with Bob and Sharon Cook and Gerry Wolf from African Leadership, flew to Nairobi. New Dawn students had planned a festive ceremony with traditional African dances, student speakers, a huge cake and a sumptuous meal. The building was designed by me and a Kenyan architect and constructed from eight high cube shipping containers.

You couldn't help but fall in love with the students of New Dawn. During the meal, we were able to sit and talk with several of them. We listened to their hopes and dreams and realized that without help they would never realize those dreams. Joyce spent time with Lucy, who wanted to be a doctor. Instead, she was admitted to one of the more prestigious teacher training colleges in Nairobi. Joyce and I decided to sponsor her university studies to become a teacher.

I had already been mentoring a group of guys. Enoch, Joseph, Martin and Francis were very likable guys and so over the years we have sponsored their education and provided financial assistance as we were able. Joseph graduated teacher training and has been teaching in a Christian school, Martin became a pastor to another slum area and started a successful Christian pre-school as part of his church, Enoch graduated from Nazarene University, 2021, in the field of social justice and community development. Enoch got a job with a child advocacy agency. Francis got a degree in aeronautical engineering with no job but has a successful Christian band. All these young adults lovingly call us mum and dad.

On my first visit to New Dawn, I met a man named Stephen. Stephen was a student, 41 years old, who had been denied an education and through sheer determination enrolled at New Dawn. The Director of the school had tried to discourage him, but he would not be dissuaded. He worked hard and graduated and wanted to study to be a pastor. Joyce and I sponsored him through four years of Bible College. He dedicated himself to his studies. I visited him on two occasions when I was in Nairobi and he was so proud to show me his room, his books and to express how happy he was to be studying to be a pastor. I was able to attend his graduation party sponsored by his brother, who was also a pastor. It was a joyous occasion. Joyce and I gave him a new Bible and a camera. When he got married, we bought two cows for his dowry. We probably have bought enough cows in Africa to have a herd larger than most farmers have.

An Amazing African Safari

Following the dedication, Joyce and I, along with Bob and Sharon Cook, went on an extended safari in two different locations of Kenya. We flew in a small prop plane from Nairobi to a dirt airstrip in the Amboseli National Park at the base of Mt. Kilimanjaro. We stayed at the Ol Tukai Lodge and did day excursions. This area is one of the largest elephant reserves in Kenya. We saw a pride of lions hunt down a wildebeest. There were rhinos, cape buffalo, giraffe, and countless species of birds and other small animals.

On our way from the airport to our camp, as we rounded a bend before crossing the river, we saw our first big cat. It was a beautiful leopard stalking a water buck and her calf. We sat and watched her as she crouched not more than 10 feet from our jeep.

After three days we flew back to Nairobi and took another flight out to the Masai Mara. One of our first adventures was a visit to a Masai village. Joyce was in a boot and had a difficult time getting around. When one of the villagers saw she was struggling to stand while the other villagers were doing their traditional welcome ceremony, he went and got her a blue plastic chair. We were standing in a barren stretch of dry dusty savannah with the circular enclosure of the village in the background. The village was a walled compound made with sticks and cow dung. All their homes inside the compound were plastered with cow dung. After a tour of the village the women brought out their wares to sell. They had all types of necklaces, bracelets and bead work of every kind. The Masai are herders and they bring their cows into the compound at night so they are safe from the wild animals. That provides plenty of fresh cow dung for plaster.

We stayed in a tent camp guarded by Masai watchmen. This was because we were staying in an unprotected area with animals all around. Any place we walked on the grounds we were escorted by the watchmen. This was no ordinary tent. It was a large tent, with a king size bed, nightstands with solar lights, luggage stands, a carpet on the floor and a wardrobe. A connecting back flap of the tent opened to a full bath with flushable toilet, a five-minute shower prepared by one of the staff and a sink with a small countertop. Out the front flap of the tent we had two stainless steel basins on a stand with a mirror. Our watchman zipped us in each

night. Each morning one of the staff would wake us, unzip the outside flap of the tent and fill the basins with hot water so we could wash up. We also had a sitting area outside with a couch and coffee table where we had hot tea brought to us every morning. Now that's the life!

The camp had a communal eating area also in an exceptionally large tent with a beautiful, polished wood table. We had our breakfast and evening meal together with others who were staying at the camp. There was no electricity, so our eating area was lit with lanterns and candles. There was also an outdoor deck overlooking the river, which was home to about 25 hippos. We had our last evening meal on the deck as the sun was setting on an unforgettable experience.

This one was probably the best safari we have ever done. We saw all the big five and a wildebeest migration and river crossing right out of National Geographic with the crocodiles snagging off the stragglers as they tried to cross the river. On the day that we did our full day bush safari we got to see a mother cheetah with her cub. She jumped on the top of a neighboring jeep full of people. She sat on the roof for quite some time looking over the landscape trying to decide which one of us in our open top jeep she was going to eat first. She was definitely looking for her next meal.

This was a special day in that we had our lunch out on the open savannah surrounded by giraffe, wildebeest, zebra and antelope. Our guide and driver found a nice shady spot under a large eucalyptus tree. Our hosts at the camp had prepared a wonderful lunch of baked chicken and all the trimmings. Our driver set up a table for us with four chairs and a table for the food. We had a white linen tablecloth, wine glasses, a nice bottle of wine, china plates, real knives and forks and cloth napkins. It was an idyllic setting and beautiful with the typical African flattop trees and animals. After this incredible experience we flew back to Nairobi and spent the night before we began out long trip home.

A Move and the Insanity of Building a House

After we arrived home, we began to make plans to move to Alabama. Alabama had experienced a killer tornado in 2010 and as we began looking for an existing home to buy, we found the housing market to be depleted because so many people who lost their homes were purchasing homes.

Matthew suggested that we consider building on a one-acre lot in Vance that he had purchased several years prior. It is on a small lake in a neighborhood that was just being developed. The major builder of other homes in the Oakridge neighborhood was Chris Liberto, a friend of Matthew's and a believer. We met with Chris and an architect who drew up our plans. We started with a basic design and began modifying from there. We got input from all our kids and each suggestion improved the plan. In January 2013 they started the site work and began building. While we were excited about making the move, we had to stop and scratch our heads and ask ourselves, "What were we thinking?" We had a beautiful home in Franklin and had some wonderful years with Melissa, Brent and their family as we watched their kids grow up. We had many opportunities to participate in their activities. We attended many baseball games, dance recitals, grandparents' days, plays and activities centered around their school. We also went to church together at Christ Community and participated in the many activities there. Now it was time to move closer to seven other grandchildren in Alabama so we could enjoy them while they were growing up and participate with them in their activities.

The new year started with a whirlwind of activity and decisions that were involved in building a house. It was difficult given the distance and the fact that we needed to be on site for a lot of those decisions. We found ourselves making many trips to Vance/Tuscaloosa from Franklin. We took turns staying with our two boys and their families. Marshall was just down the road, a few miles from the building site. Our builder estimated about five months to completion and he was awfully close; we moved in on June 3. Our new home is situated on an acre of lakefront property with an expanse of sloping green lawn to the lake that provides us with a peaceful sanctuary. We love living here except for the distance to doctors and shopping, it is comforting to know that we have no mortgage. God was good to us in that we didn't even have to put our house in Franklin on the market. A single woman from church learned we were moving and wanted to see our house. After she came back and looked at it several times, she decided to make an offer and we accepted. It was a blessing not to have more decisions to add on top of a basket that was already full.

Just before we moved, Brandon graduated from CPA. Brandon graduated with a baseball scholarship to Lincoln Memorial University, which gave him the opportunity to play ball all four years of college. Who would have thought that the little guy we watched play so many games at Jim Warren Park would end up winning pitcher for his college division championship?

Our 50ᵗʰ Wedding Anniversary

For our 50ᵗʰ anniversary, our whole family went to Destin, Florida to celebrate. Melissa and her family were late in arriving because of the unfortunate death of Michael's closest friend David Taff. We were staying in the house in Destin that belonged to David's family. It was hard for Michael because he had stayed there many times with David. We had a wonderful time. Marshall had put together a historic showing of slides. I think he had a cassette for each one of our four kids, plus family adventures. We took family photos and had fun at the beach. Melissa had put together a scrapbook full of pictures and memories.

On our actual anniversary I rented a limo to pick Joyce and me up at the house and take us to Cypress Inn for dinner. After dinner, all five of the young whippersnappers met us at Cypress Inn and rode home with us in the limo. They were ecstatic with the adventure as our driver took us on a tour of Tuscaloosa. Of course, they had to push every button they could find and get drinks from the onboard fridge.

Back to Africa – Out of Africa

In September, I went to Malawi for African Leadership and the Peoples Church in Franklin. I had been working on the project at Adziwa Christian school for several years and the school had progressed to the point that the staff needed some serious training. The new principal, Christian, requested that I spend three full days with his teachers helping them understand a biblical perspective in teaching. Since I didn't know these teachers or their biblical background and understanding, I started with the basic elements of the faith. Things like salvation, grace and the sacrifice of Christ on the cross. I basically shared that unless they had a relationship with Jesus and saw the world from a biblical perspective, they would never be able to teach their students from a biblical worldview. I had a growing sense that the Holy Spirit was at work, so at the close of the last session I gave them an opportunity to come to the front of the room if they wanted to receive Jesus or renew their commitment to him. Three of the teachers came up and said they wanted to receive Jesus as their Savior and two others wanted to renew their commitment. This was at the beginning of their new school year and Christian emailed me well into the year to say it was the best year they had ever had.

After a day of rest, I started two days of training with the board of the school. This was a difficult assignment! A couple of the board members didn't show up, there was open hostility on the part of a couple of members who were there and besides that I was starting to get a severe pain in my back and side. I didn't know what it was, so I persevered through the first day. During the night the pain was so bad I didn't know what to do. I called Joyce and cried on the phone to her. Not sure what good I thought that would do. She prayed for me over the phone. When morning came, I told Karen Stapel, who was traveling with me, that I couldn't continue. She got our local host, Christian to come and get me in his van and take me to a clinic. Well, what a place, just a slight cut above a grass hut with a witch doctor. It was dark, dirty and ill equipped. I stayed the night in a room with water running down the wall and slept on a bed that made me hurt worse. They gave me a little bell to ring if I needed someone. Every time I was awake there was this little nurse with a heavy coat and hood standing beside my bed praying for me.

The next morning, one of the local missionaries along with a doctor from a mission hospital came to get me. When I tried to thank the people at the clinic for the little nurse who stayed with me all night, they said there wasn't any such person like that in the clinic. Hmm, an angel perhaps? This was another case of Gods providential care and FAITHFULNESS. *"For he will command his angels concerning you to guard you in all your ways".* Psalm 91:11 NIV

The doctor at the mission hospital was from New Zealand and after an examination she decided that I had the shingles. By this time, it was too late to take the medicine for Shingles as it had been several days into the process. I was hurting so bad that they gave me pain shots every three hours. Once I was good enough to leave the hospital, I got word from Joyce that Arnie Trillet, our good friend from Colorado Springs, was getting on a flight to come and assist me on my journey home. I was so weak that there was no way I could travel by myself and the medical airlift flights were too expensive. First, I had to get back to South Africa to get my flight to the US. Flights out of Lilongwe, Malawi to JoBerg were all full for three weeks. I had missed the flight I was supposed to be on.

With a lot of prayer and a miracle working FAITHFUL God, I finally got the last seat, first class, on the plane my friend Arnie came in on. That meant that Arnie had to wait in Lilongwe for two days for his return flight to JoBerg. Karen and he had a good time as she took him around Lilongwe to see the sights. He said he had a better time without me being there. Anna Marie Russell, ACSI Director for South Africa, met me at the airport in JoBerg and took me to her home to rest and wait for Arnie. I was able to work with Delta to secure two business class seats for the trip home. That's the only way I could have made it. They had a wheelchair waiting for me in all the airports: JoBerg, Amsterdam, Atlanta and Birmingham. Arnie wheeled me through each airport to our next gate. Arnie stayed with us for a couple of days before heading back to Colorado Springs. Arnie is a dear friend and certainly a good Samaritan in getting me out of Africa.

An interesting side note on Malawi: on my first trip to Malawi the Central Baptist Church, the African Leadership partner on the ground, assigned me a young man, Sothini Banda, to be my driver. Consequently, he was my driver on every trip I made. His wife came up missing between a couple of my trips and he wrote to say that her father had taken her home because Sothini had never paid the bride price to his father-in-law for her. The father-in-law wanted four cows. Sothini only had money enough saved for two cows so we sent him the money to buy two more cows. He got his wife home and she became pregnant with twins. She gave birth to two healthy baby boys but didn't have enough breast milk for them So we helped them buy formula to help as a supplement for the two little guys. We keep in contact Sothini.

Loss of Dear Friends

Two of our absolute best friends went home to be with Jesus in 2014. Our dear friend and missionary colleague Ken Foster ran into the arms of Jesus. Ken was a runner so I'm sure he didn't walk. Also, our dear sweet friend Margaret McIlhenny from Belfast, Northern Ireland, went to be with her Jesus. We had traveled to Northern Ireland on two occasions where we stayed with them and they had been to our home as well. On one trip to visit us, we took them to Fairhaven in East Tennessee and travelled around the Appalachian Mountains. We had such good times together. One time we were in Belfast over April 1st, at breakfast we always had tea. I put my usual two teaspoons of sugar in my cup, but when I took my first sip, I quickly learned that Margaret had switched the sugar for salt. When I made a face, she shouted, "April Fools!" and we all laughed like fools. We loved driving around Northern Ireland with them. We visited castles, the Waterford crystal plant, and of course there was the Giant's causeway, a natural phenomenon along the North Sea. On the day we visited there were gale force winds blowing and it was raining sideways.

Starting our Next 50 Years with a Cruise and a Nyack Class Reunion

In August I surprised Joyce with a seven-day Caribbean cruise aboard the Royal Caribbean Anthem of the Seas. This trip was for our 51st wedding anniversary. We sailed from Ft. Lauderdale to the southern Caribbean to the Bahamas, St. Martin and St. Thomas. We enjoyed the evening shows, the food and our balcony room with a view of the interior promenade. We swam, ate a lot and just enjoyed the opulence of the ship. We enjoyed the beautiful blue waters of St. Thomas.

Our graduating class from Nyack celebrated our 50th class reunion as part of the annual Nyack homecoming. Bob and Sharon Cook, Jean Clayton and Joyce and I put a lot of planning into it and with the help of the Alumni office hyped it up as the "great confession." Seven of us guys had been involved in removing the bell from the belfry of Pardington Hall, the school chapel. It was a challenge from our class sponsor to find something to create a rivalry between the junior and senior classes. He felt our campus was dull. He didn't suggest the bell, but in a bull session we decided it could be a great rivalry, and it didn't disappoint. At one time we hid the bell in the attic of our apartment and another time in a pile of leaves behind the flower shop where we worked. This rivalry went on long after we left Nyack. Dr. Boon was our college President and it would really grate on him every time we drove an old pickup past his home at 3am ringing the bell. The following day he was more of a grouch than normal. It was a constant game of cat and mouse between the juniors and seniors.

For the 50th celebration, classmates had written poems, we had noise makers in the shape of a bell, we sang the song, *Who Stole the Chapel Bell* and then we had the big reveal and confession. No one for 50 years had known who was responsible for this dastardly deed. There was a good group from our class who attended the celebration. We had a great time renewing friendships that we had only been able to keep long distance since many of us had been missionaries scattered around the world.

Graduations Galore

2015 was the year of graduations. Ava graduated from Kindergarten at ACA, Michelle graduated from high school and Michael graduated from Mississippi State. He started in a one-year master's program that same year.

Michelle graduated from Independence High School in Franklin with an emphasis on Fashion Design. For her senior project, she had to create a clothing line that was modeled at a school fashion show. It was quite an exciting evening. She went on to Mississippi State in the fall and majored in Fashion Design and Marketing. We attended a couple of the fashion shows that Michelle had helped produce.

I continued to travel for African Leadership. I went to Uganda where I conducted a board training for the leadership and potential board members of Uganda. South Sudan and Ethiopia. Following the board training I went on to Kenya to work with the leadership of New Dawn.

Awards, Travels and a Wedding!

Samuel graduated from Briarwood High School in 2016 and had received his Eagle Scout Award. Both were impressive ceremonies and we were enormously proud of him. He enrolled at Samford University.

It was a very exciting to see our first grandchild married. Our whole family was in attendance as Michael married Elizabeth Zampini in a very impressive ceremony. We enjoyed the great food and dancing at the reception.

In July we took Brock, our sixth grandchild, to Guatemala. We were hosted by Stuart and Sheny Salazar. They introduced Brock to the work of ACSI in Latin America and shared the story of our involvement in the starting of the office. We were humbled to hear them share what we had meant to them over the years. We took Brock to visit a project on the dump where kids and their parents scavenged for anything that could be sold for meager earnings. It was called the Potter's House. We were able to see the mounds of plastics and metal that they had bundled for resale. There were classrooms for schooling for the kids.

We visited two Christian schools in poor communities and Brock got to visit in the classrooms. He was like a Rockstar. We also took him to visit the orphanage at New Life Advance International, one of Grace Church's mission partners. We toured the orphanage and the school. Brock passed out candy to some of the kids. He was an immediate hit and all the girls had eyes for him.

We traveled to Antigua and Lake Atitlan where we spent the night. We visited the market and took a boat ride to some of the little villages along the lake where Brock did some shopping for gifts to take home. He and Stuart really enjoyed swimming in the big pool at the hotel.

In August we drove to Branson, Missouri for a reunion with ACSI colleagues who were all retired. We stopped in Memphis and stayed with Steve and Diane for the night to break up the trip. I slipped in their bathtub while taking a shower and broke four ribs, but we didn't let that stop us. In great pain I drove on to Branson. We enjoyed many of the activities and especially the Sight and Sound theater for the show "Moses". The activity we enjoyed most was seeing old friends and having close fellowship with them. Little did we realize that this would be the last time we would see some of them this side of heaven.

In September I flew to South Africa to lead the International Board meeting of OSWW. We had our meeting at a beautiful seaside resort on the Indian Ocean. These were watershed meetings and set in motion the process of finding a mission that we could partner with.

In October Joyce and I flew to Zanesville along with Steve for the 75th anniversary celebration of the C&MA Church. Our grandmother Renicks was one of the founding members of the church and mom and dad had been active members until they left Zanesville. Joyce and I had also been active members and were commissioned in the church for missionary service to Ecuador. Steve and I had grown up in the church. We participated through music, where Steve played the piano and I played the organ. We were active in the youth group. In the early 70s Joyce had been the founder and Director of the Wee Pals Nursery school, a ministry of the church.

Joyce and I stayed around for a few extra days so I could see as many of my cousins as possible. We were able to catch up with five of them that I hadn't seen in many years. Then we took the Greyhound bus and went to Butler. Joyce's bother Dale picked us up in Pittsburg and we spent two weeks with Joyce's family. Joyce and her two sisters, Beve and Debbie, had a sister's day. They drove to Meadville for breakfast at Cracker Barrel, then they ended up shopping at an upscale mall in Pittsburgh where they had dinner before returning to Butler. They made it a day. We flew from Pittsburgh back to Birmingham.

I continued to work with Vanderbilt in 2017 on a possible kidney transplant. I agreed to accept a Hepatitis B donor so they required that I have a heart catheterization. When the results came back, it showed blockage so to have a kidney transplant, I had to have open heart surgery to clear the blockage. I had the surgery at UAB Birmingham and recovered quickly. The downside is that they started me on dialysis. I sure didn't like going to the dialysis center three times a week, so as quickly as possible I transitioned to PD home dialysis. While it was freeing, it required yet another surgery. I had to have a port placed in my stomach by which to hook up to the dialysis machine. This required that I had to do four fills and four drains every night. While it was all automatic while I slept, it was still very confining. I still have good kidney function so they graduated me off the machine to one manual bag per night.

While I was in the hospital, Brandon graduated from Lincoln Memorial University in May. Unfortunately, we were unable to attend. Brandon moved back to Franklin and started work.

Alan McIlhenny came from Ireland and Vern and Bevan Howard came from Texas to check on me and make sure I was still alive. Vern helped me all the nights they were here to set up my dialysis machine.

We held a mini whippersnapper camp, and this brought the era of whippersnapper camps to a close. Since I wasn't up to a lot of rowdy activity, Michaela came and helped and we played it low key.

Travel for me was restricted and came to a screeching halt. We didn't go anywhere in 2018. Elijah got his Eagle Scout award and graduated from Briarwood Christian High School with honors. He enrolled at Samford University.

It was a lean year for any activity involving us. Brock was running varsity track for ACA by this time and playing in the band. Carson, Will, Jackson and Ava were playing basketball so we were involved in going to as many of their gams as possible.

A Year of Celebrations

Wedding bells were ringing once again. Brandon married Meredith Roman on a beautiful March day in 2019. It was an outdoor wedding at a beautiful wedding venue in Franklin. The pergola where they were married was set against a lake. Meredith's four brothers provided the music. When Brandon and Meredith were pronounced husband and wife, they raised their hands and raced down the aisle with great exuberance. As it began to get dark, we all moved inside to a sit-down dinner and an evening of dancing. Oh, what fun.

Michelle graduated from Mississippi State University with her degree in fashion design and marketing. Michael and Elizabeth met us just outside the arena going into Michelle's graduation ceremony to tell us that we were going to be great grandparents. How many happys can you take all in one day? It was hard to pick Michelle out from among the hundreds of gradates. We went out to eat following the graduation. Of course, it was a Mexican restaurant. Where else would Michelle choose? Michelle was able to find a job in Tupelo, Mississippi at Blue Delta Jeans Company, a custom jeans manufacturer. Now she, a Jean, is making jeans for the rich and famous.

Then on November 22, 2019, Mackenzie Ann Jean was born. Wow! Our first great grandchild. Another happy time to celebrate in 2019. We got another little girl in the family. We were so excited that we made the trip to Franklin to see her right after Thanksgiving. It was a special treat to have the four generation of our family together for the first time.

We are closing this off at the end of 2020. This has been a difficult year for everyone but we are THANKFUL that God has brought us through.

2020 is not a year we want to write about, only to say that it is a year that we could never have imagined. We had never experienced a worldwide pandemic. We are still scratching our heads trying to respond to all the changes that we are dealing with as a result. Who could have predicted that we would see the whole world locked down, people wearing masks and having to stay at a six-foot social distance from family and friends?

We lost some very close friends during this yea; our former boss, Dr. Paul Kienel, longtime Quito friend Tommy Berry our Open Schools Worldwide board chairperson, Vivian Subramoney, South Africa and our brother-in-law Tom Morton. Our Hearts were deeply saddened and we grieved along with their families. We have been locked in at home for most of the year with the exception of a week in Gatlinburg with Steve and Diane to celebrate our anniversaries. Samuel Leonard proposed to Bethany White and wedding bells will be ringing in May 2021. Another bright spot was that Mackenzie Ann, our great granddaughter came to visit us in February before COVID hit.

Joyce and I have enjoyed reminiscing about the past 70-plus years of our lives. We have relived many of the historic events of our 78 years, the ancestorial history of our two families, the ups and downs and ebb and flow that life has given us. We have had many opportunities to lean on God and in every circumstance have found him FAITHFUL. We hope you, our family, will see through the pages of this book the great spiritual heritage that you have and the wonderful legacy that those who have gone before you have left. Yours is the privilege and responsibility to continue that God given legacy for your children and your children's children for generations to come. As you walk the journey of life, we hope you will take time to record it as an addendum to these pages.

One final thought is captured in the words of a favorite hymn penned by Thomas O. Chisholm, Great Is Thy Faithfulness based on the scripture from Lamentations 3:22-23 RSV, *"The steadfast love of the Lord never ceases, his mercies never come to an end; they are new every morning; great is your faithfulness."*

Great is Thy faithfulness, O God my Father;
There is no shadow of turning with Thee;
Thou changest not, Thy compassions, they fail not;
As Thou hast been, Thou forever will be.

Summer and winter and springtime and harvest,
Sun, moon and stars in their courses above
Join with all nature in manifold witness
To Thy great faithfulness, mercy and love.

Pardon for sin and a peace that endureth
Thine own dear presence to cheer and to guide;
Strength for today and bright hope for tomorrow,
Blessings all mine, with ten thousand beside!

[Chorus]
Great is Thy faithfulness!
Great is Thy faithfulness!
Morning by morning new mercies I see.
All I have needed Thy hand hath provided;
Great is Thy faithfulness, Lord, unto me.

Printed in the United States
by Baker & Taylor Publisher Services